W9-DFR-606

ANCIENT GREECE

DR. ANTON POWELL

THIRD EDITION

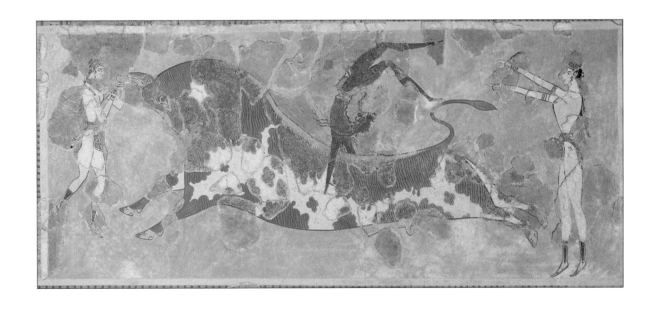

CHELSEA HOUSE
PUBLISHERS
An imprint of Infobase Publishing

Cultural Atlas for Young People
ANCIENT GREECE
Third Edition

Copyright © 2007 The Brown Reference Group plc

Chelsea House
An imprint of Infobase Publishing
132 West 31st Street
New York, NY 10001

Library of Congress Cataloging-in-Publication Data available upon request.

ISBN: 0-8160-6821-6

ISBN 13 digit: 978-0-8160-6821-0

Set ISBN: 978-0-8160-7218-7

3380

Chelsea House books are available at special discounts when purchased in bulk quantities for businesses, associations, institutions, or sales promotions. Please call our Special Sales Department in New York at (212) 967-8800 or (800) 322-8755.

You can find Chelsea House on the World Wide Web at:
http://www.chelseahouse.com

The Brown Reference Group
(incorporating Andromeda Oxford Limited)
8 Chapel Place, Rivington Street
London EC2A 3DQ
www.brownreference.com

For The Brown Reference Group plc:
Editorial Director: Lindsey Lowe
Project Editor: Graham Bateman
Editor: Virginia Carter
Design: Steve McCurdy
Senior Managing Editor: Tim Cooke

Printed in Singapore

10 9 8 7 6 5 4 3 2 1

Artwork and Picture Credits

All site plans by Oxford Illustrators. All maps by Lovell Johns, Oxford.
Color artwork by Kevin Maddison and Chris Forsey; other artwork by Peter Chesterton.

Key: t = top, b = bottom, c = center, l = left, r = right

Title page D.A. Harissiadis, Athens. 5 ZEFA. 8/9 ZEFA. 10bl, 13 EA. 14 DAI, Athens. 15t Arte e Immagini srl/ CORBIS. 15b Araldo de Luca/CORBIS. 17, 21t, 21b Scala, Florence. 22 Giraudon, Paris. 23t EA. 24 DAI, Rome. 25tl EA. 25b Clive Spong. 25cl JF. 25tc Kunsthistorisches Museum, Vienna. 25tr Museum of Corfu. 26/27 Wolfgang Kaehler/CORBIS. 27tl Louvre, Paris. 30 Malcolm McGregor, London. 33tl Staatliche Museum, West Berlin. 33b EA. 36/37, 38t BM. 38bl JF. 39bc Pergamon Museum, East Berlin. 39r JF. 41t BM. 41b EA. 42 Phaidon Archives. 43t The Art Archive/ Dagli Orti. 43b Malcolm McGregor. 44/45, 45tr, 45c, 45b ST. 47cl National Museum, Copenhagen. 47bl JF. 47br DAFA. 48/49 Zefa Picture Library, London. 49 Capitoline Museum, Rome. 50/51 Wolfgang Kaehler/CORBIS 60t Robert Haas, London. 60b D.A. Harissiadis, Athens. 61l EA. 61tr Hirmer Fotoarchiv, Munich. 62 Edward Dodwell. 62/63, 63tr EA. 63cr Robert Harding Associates, London. 63br JF. 64t Ash. 64bl Museum of Fine Arts, Boston, Mass. 64/65, 65t Scala, Florence. 65b Richard and Adam Hook. 66t Hirmer Fotoarchiv, Munich. 66b R.V. Schoder, S.J., Chicago. 67tl Mansell Collection, London. 67tr EA. 67cr Hirmer Fotoarchiv, Munich. 67b Alison Frantz. 68 A.F. Kersting, London. 69 Staatliche Museum, Berlin. 70t R.V. Schoder, S.J., Chicago. 71tl Alison Frantz. 71tr Edwin Smith, Saffron Walden. 71b Hirmer Fotoarchiv, Munich. 73t, 73cl EA. 73bl MH. 73bc Zefa Picture Library, London. 73br SH. 74t MH. 74b SH. 75t, 75b Robert Harding Associates, London. 78, 79b, 80tl, 80tr, 80bl MH. 81b Scala, Florence. 83tr Museum of Fine Arts, Boston, Mass. 83cr Scala, Florence. 83br Louvre, Paris. 84 Wadsworth Atheneum, Hartford, Conn.;

J. Pierpont Morgan Collection. 86tr EA. 86bl BM. 87t Louvre, Paris. 88bl EA. 88br Metropolitan Museum of Art, NY, Rogers Fund, 1913. 88/89 R. Barnard, Somerset and JF. 89br BM. 92 Zefa Picture Library, London.

List of Abbreviations
Ash = Ashmolean Museum, Oxford;
BM = British Museum, London;
DAI = Deutsches Archäologisches Institut;
DAFA = Délégation Archéologique Française en Afghanistan; EA = Ekdotike Athenon, Athens; JF = John Fuller, Cambridge; MH = Michael Holford, Loughton; SH = Sonia Halliday, Weston Turville, Bucks; ST = Spyros Tsardavoglou, Athens.

Contents

Introduction

THIS BOOK IS ABOUT THE ANCIENT GREEKS. THEY WERE perhaps the most restless, adventurous, and creative people who have ever lived. In ancient times Greek towns and villages stretched far beyond the small country we now know as Greece. In the late fourth century B.C.E. Alexander the Great, with his Greek-speaking troops, conquered a territory from Asia Minor and Egypt in the west to India in the east.

Our book is an atlas. Its maps will help you keep track of what Greeks in different places were doing. The maps also show how the landscape of Greece shaped the way Greeks lived. To understand the Greeks, maps are even more important than they are for most other civilizations. Greece, for most of its long history, had no capital city and no single government. Instead, there were dozens, sometimes even hundreds, of independent Greek communities. These are called "city-states." But probably only two of them, Athens and Alexandria, grew as big as a modern city.

If we could travel back through time and visit a typical Greek community, it would seem to us more like a village than a city. Yet a large village in ancient Greece often had its own defensive wall, and made its own decisions on big issues, such as whether to go to war. The independence of these communities probably helped their citizens feel that their views mattered. This self-confidence encouraged many Greeks to be creative.

The ideas of the Greeks spread very widely. From the second century B.C.E. most Greek communities were eventually taken into the empire of Rome. But so clever and educated were many Greeks that they found themselves educating their Roman masters. They taught the Romans how to write, paint, build, and even how to run the Roman Empire. Today the Greeks are definitely in fashion. This is because there is great respect for new ideas, and Greece excelled in producing new ideas that would last. "Drama," "athletics," "philosophy," "democracy" are all words of Greek origin for things that were invented by the ancient Greeks.

Our book looks at the most famous periods of ancient Greek history, from 1600 B.C.E. (the late Bronze Age) down to around 100 B.C.E., the time of the Roman conquest. In this long stretch of time, Greek civilization took strikingly different forms. For example, Mycenaean Greeks of the Bronze Age are famous for their beautiful paintings and metalwork, and for the script in which they wrote—Linear B. By the eighth century B.C.E., the Greeks had forgotten Linear B. Instead, they used a very different script, the first letters of which were *alpha* and *beta*, the basis of the alphabet that we use today.

Ancient Greece is divided into two main sections. The first, **A History of Greece**, builds up the story of the Greeks and tells how they gradually became an important world power. Throughout this section there are maps illustrating themes or topics in the main text. Many of them are accompanied by charts giving important dates and events in Greek history. The second part, **Culture and Society**, looks at the effect the Greeks had on the lands they occupied. At the beginning of this section are maps that are more typically atlaslike, containing details of rivers, towns, mountains, and lowlands. Important Greek towns and villages, with their ancient Greek names, can be located on these maps using the Gazetteer on page 94.

Our story of *Ancient Greece* is arranged in double-page spreads. Each spread is a complete story. So you can either read the book from beginning to end, or just dip into it to learn about a specific topic. The Glossary on page 93 explains historical and Greek terms used in the book.

Abbreviations used in this book

B.C.E. = Before Common Era (also known as B.C.). C.E. = Common Era (also known as A.D.). c. = *circa* (about).

in = inch; ft = foot; mi = mile.

cm = centimeter; m = meter; km = kilometer.

When referring to dates, early third century B.C.E., for example, means about 290 or 280 B.C.E., and late third century B.C.E. means about 220 or 210 B.C.E.

The spelling of Greek names adopted in this book uses the *k* form (with -os and -on endings) rather than the alternative *c* form (with -us and -um endings) where appropriate.

▶ Copies of the Karyatids of the Erechtheion on the Akropolis, the citadel of ancient Athens (the originals are in a museum in Athens).

Timelines

	2000 B.C.E.	1500 B.C.E	1000 B.C.E	800 B.C.E	600 B.C.E
CULTURAL PERIOD	Bronze age		Dark age	Archaic period	
AEGEAN AND GREEK MAINLAND	Cretan palace civilization / Shaft graves at Mycenae / Explosion at Santorini / Fall of Knossos / Fall of Mycenaeans		Iron introduced from East then return to bronze	Population increases in Greece / Rise of aristocratic families / Chief period of colonization to E and W / International festivals established / Tyrants in control of many cities / Invention of hoplite fighting	First Greek coins / Beginnings of democracy at Athens / Sparta dominates Peloponnese
POTTERY STYLE ART AND ARCHITECTURE	Great palaces in Crete / Figurines, fine working in gold and semiprecious stones (e.g. sealstones)	Santorini frescoes / Great beehive tombs	Sub-Mycenaean protogeometric	Geometric / Orientalizing / Monumental vases / Olympia tripods / First stone temples	Archaic (Athenian Black Figure) / Kouroi and korai
LITERATURE, PHILOSOPHY, AND SCIENCE		Linear A tablets / Linear B tablets / Phoenician alphabet		Greek alphabet / Homer / Hesiod / Lyric poets	Beginnings of tragedy and comedy / Pythagoras / Sappho
EGYPT, ASIA MINOR, AND THE EAST	Hittite Empire in Anatolia / Babylonian Empire	Egyptian New Kingdom / Great temples / Tutankhamon	Greek colonies in Ionia, then around Black Sea	Assyrian Empire at most powerful / Assyrians lose power to Medes and Babylonians	Darius founds Persian Empire / Persians conquer Egypt

So-called mask of Agamemnon from Mycenae, 1550–1500 B.C.E.

The "warrior vase" from Mycenae, early 12th century B.C.E.

Geometric amphora from Athens, c.750 B.C.E.

The "peplos kore" from the Athenian Akropolis, c.530 B.C.E.

Octopus flask from eastern Crete, 1350 B.C.E.

13th-century B.C.E carved ivory from Mycenae.

Bronze statue of hoplite, Dodone.

Classical period	Hellenistic period	Roman Empire	Byzantine Empire

Persian invasions

Athens dominates Delian League

Age of Perikles

Peloponnesian War

Athenian revival

Rise of Macedon

Fall of Sparta

Campaigns of Alexander

Rise to power of Achaean and Aetolian leagues

Macedonian wars

Macedonia becomes Roman province

Achaea becomes Roman province

Greece remains cultural and intellectual center of Mediterranean

The Parthenon at Athens, completed 441–432 B.C.E.

Alexander the Great at the battle of Issos. Detail from the "Alexander mosaic" found at Pompeii, copy of a Greek painting c.300 B.C.E.

The Venus de Milo, a second-century B.C.E marble statue from Melos.

Roman coin of Hadrian, second century C.E.

Athenian Red Figure   South Italian painters

Temple of Zeus at Olympia

Parthenon, Erechtheion

Pheidias and Polykleitos (sculptors)

Polygnotos (painter)

Praxiteles (sculptor)

Mausoleum at Halikarnassos

Hellenistic baroque

Altar of Zeus, Pergamon

Winged Victory of Samothrace

Venus de Milo

Santa Sophia built Constantinople (Istanbul)

Roman copying of Greek sculpture and architecture

Fifth-century B.C.E vase with archaic poets, Sappho and Alkaios.

Silver coin from Athens, c.440 B.C.E.

Painted terracotta, women gossiping, c.320 B.C.E.

Bust of philosopher, possibly Bion.

Aischylos, Pindar, Sophokles, Herodotos, Euripides, Sokrates, Hippokrates, Thucydides, Aristophanes

Plato, Aristotle, Epicurus, Theokritos, Euclid, Archimedes

Creation of library at Alexandria

Pausanias

Darius crosses Hellespont and invades Greece

Alexander conquers Asia Minor, Egypt, Persia, NW India

Successor kingdoms, Ptolemaic, Seleukid dynasties

Gauls settle in Galatia (modern Turkey)

Parthian Empire founded

Rome defeats Antiochos of Syria

Pergamon becomes Roman province

Egypt becomes Roman province

Sasanian Empire founded in Persia

Byzantion refounded by Romans (Constantinople)

Part One

A History of Greece

▲ A young fisherman. Seashells, flying fish, and octopuses also attracted the attention of Theran artists.

▶ Amphitheater at Dodone, built 297–272 B.C.E. It seated 14,000 spectators.

Minoans and Mycenaeans

THE FIRST GREAT CIVILIZATION OF THE Aegean world was the Minoan, on the island of Crete. It was in its prime between about 2200 and 1450 B.C.E. Its rulers were probably not Greek-speaking.

The most famous palace of the Minoans was at Knossos (see pages 60–61). Here many elegant rooms had wall paintings showing the beautiful women of the royal court. In one painting young people are leaping and doing somersaults between the horns of a bull.

The Minoan civilization seems to have been mainly a peaceful one. Its wealth came from farming on Crete and from trade with Syria, Egypt, and the Greek mainland.

The Mycenaean kingdoms

Around 1450 B.C.E. Crete fell into the power of Greek speakers—people called the Mycenaeans. Writing found by archaeologists on clay tablets at Knossos has been deciphered as Greek: the script is known as Linear B. Many similar tablets with this script have been found on the Greek mainland. They tell us what was in the storehouses of the palaces, and how wealth was distributed.

The best known of the mainland palaces were at Mycenae and Pylos (see pages 62–63). Between about 1600 and 1150 B.C.E., Greece probably contained several independent little kingdoms. The name Mycenaean is given to them all.

Mycenaean artists and craftsmen borrowed many styles from the Minoan civilization. But the Mycenaean way of life seems to have been more warlike. Tall warrior kings drove in chariots to battle or to go hunting for lions and boars.

The craftsmen and builders of Mycenaean palaces did superb work. They used huge stones to make defensive walls and vast underground tombs for their rulers. In later times Greeks could not understand how these stones had been lifted. They thought that the walls of Mycenae were built by giants.

Trade with other lands

The wealth of Mycenaean Greece was created not only by farmers and craftsmen but also by traders who brought goods from remote lands. Papyrus, the ancestor of paper, was imported from Egypt. Amber, used in jewelry such as necklaces, rings, and pendants, came from the coast of the Baltic Sea, far away in northern Europe.

◀ This arched corridor of massive stones is part of the fortress of Tiryns. It lies between Mycenae and the coast, and was probably built to block raids on Mycenae by invaders from overseas.

▶ The Aegean Sea in the Bronze Age. Crete, in the south, was the home of the Minoan civilization, which the Greeks of the mainland both conquered and copied. Mycenae, on the southern part of the mainland, has left spectacular ruins from the late second millennium B.C.E. (c.1300 B.C.E.). But many other Greek towns, such as Pylos, Sparta, and Gla, may have been independent of the gold-rich kings of Mycenae.

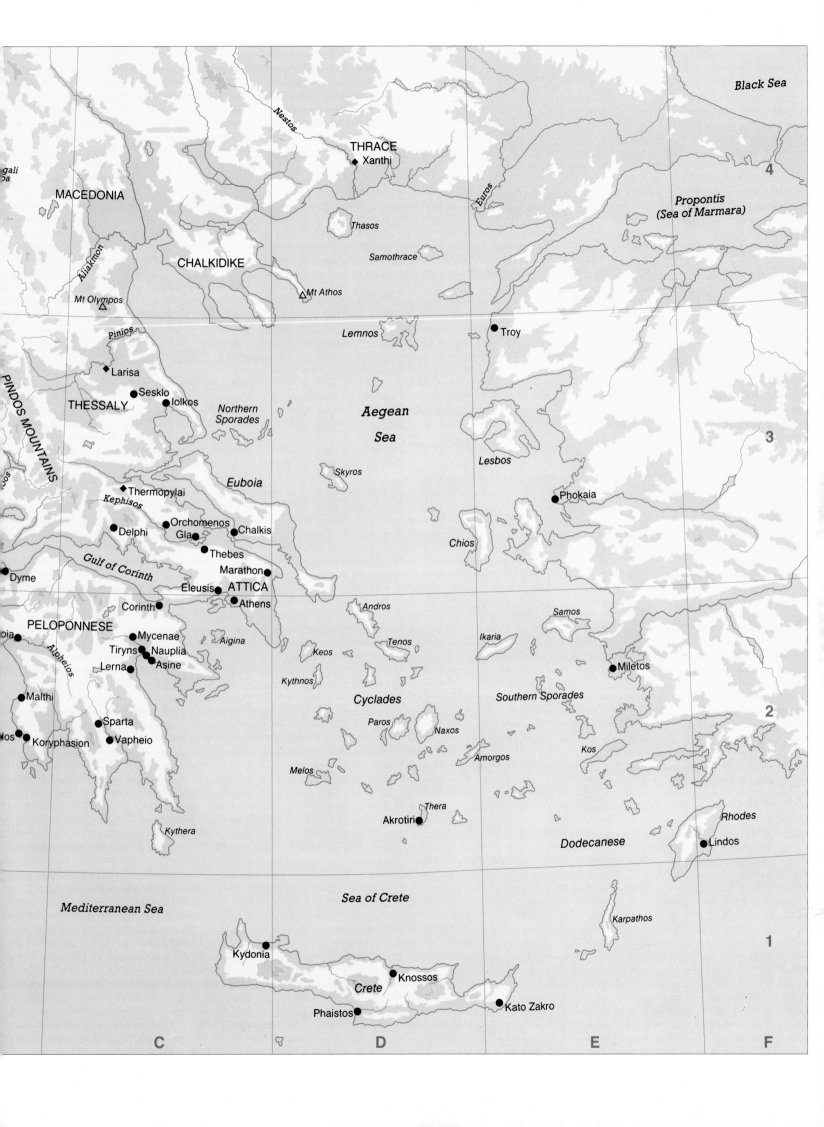

The Dark Age: Homer's Greece

AFTER THE FALL OF THE MYCENAEAN palaces, Greece entered a dark age. Little is known about this period of the country's history. Archaeology reveals that grand building and fine craftsmanship ceased. Trade was probably disrupted, with a resulting increase in poverty.

Yet Greeks of the dark age did at least one thing superbly. They remembered many details about the bygone Mycenaean civilization and worked them into long stories of adventure. These were in verse. Two of them survive, told and retold over the centuries until they took their final form. It is thought that they were shaped by a poet named

Homer in the mid-eighth century B.C.E. These poems are the *Iliad* and the *Odyssey* (see also pages 14–15 and 64–65).

From about 1200 to 1150 B.C.E. the Mycenaean world was under attack. No one knows who its enemies were, however. One Linear B tablet from Pylos (see page 10) records that men were stationed on the coast as lookouts, so it is possible that the attackers came by sea.

The mighty walls at Mycenae itself were probably built against such enemies. They may seem a sign of strength, but in reality the walls marked the growing weakness of Mycenae. At the height of its power the

▼ Places of importance in the dark age of ancient Greece. Emigrants were colonizing the western coast of Asia Minor. Some signs of life survived in the great centers of the Mycenaean past, such as Tiryns, Sparta, and Mycenae itself. Geometric pottery (see page 80) was made throughout Greece at this time.

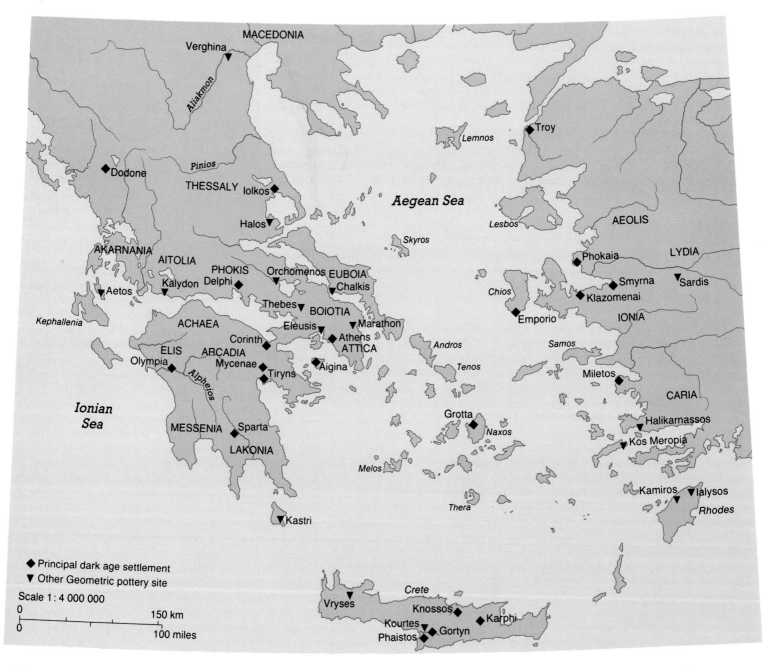

♦ Principal dark age settlement
▼ Other Geometric pottery site

Scale 1 : 4 000 000

0 — 150 km
0 — 100 miles

palace had needed no such protection. Mycenae, Pylos, and other palaces were captured and burned. Never again was Mycenae to have such great power.

Remembering the Mycenaean age

Dark-age poets remembered that there had once been royal palaces at Mycenae, Pylos, and also at a place in northwestern Asia Minor named Troy. They knew that Mycenae had been rich in gold and that Mycenaean metalworkers had made many wonderful treasures.

The *Iliad* tells of armies from Mycenae, Pylos, and elsewhere that fought against Troy and besieged the fortress for 10 years (see page 14). The picture which the poem gives of Mycenaean weapons and styles of fighting may well be roughly correct.

The *Iliad* also tells of aristocratic leaders, such as Odysseus and Diomedes, Achilles, Aias (Ajax), and Menelaos, who fight enemy chieftains in one-to-one combat. They use "tower-tall" shields, kill by throwing spears, and travel to and from the fighting on chariots.

These accounts are very different from what we known about the main style of land-fighting in the later, classical period. Then soldiers marched into battle in long, relatively disciplined lines carrying smaller, round shields and spears that were for stabbing, not throwing. Archaeology has shown that the Mycenaean aristocracy did indeed use chariots. The "tower-tall" shields are illustrated beautifully on the Mycenaean dagger blade shown above.

The people in the dark age who listened to the poems about the Trojan War may not themselves have been very warlike. Again and again in the *Iliad*, fighting is compared with scenes from quiet country life. Shepherds, woodcutters, and fishermen seem to have been more familiar figures than soldiers. So the *Iliad* tells us not only about the world of Mycenae but also about daily life in the dark age afterwards.

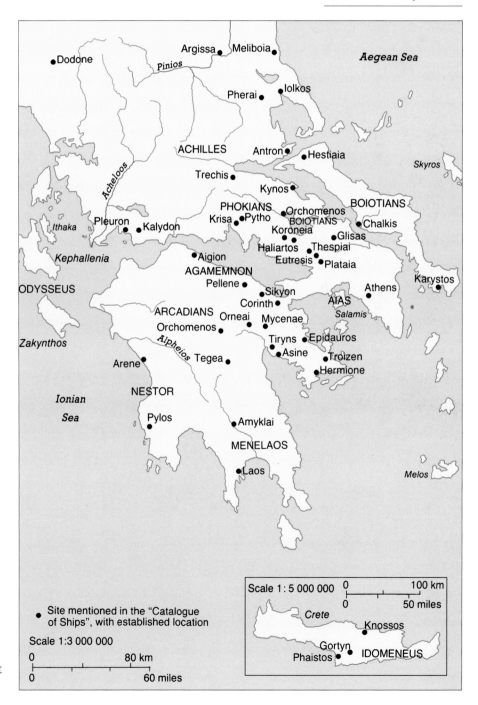

The Siege of Troy

O N THE NORTHWESTERN TIP OF ASIA
Minor was a fortress named Troy (or Ilion).
Archaeologists now think it was attacked
around 1270 B.C.E. Unusually, large numbers of
storage pots have been found at Troy in ruined
houses from that time. These suggest that the
inhabitants had laid in supplies for a siege. Perhaps
this was the war that gave birth to the *Iliad*, the long
tale of an episode during a siege of Troy. The *Iliad*
may correctly record historical details, but it is
also a lively historical novel in verse.

Queen Helen of Troy
The *Iliad* and the *Odyssey* tell of Queen Helen.
Extremely beautiful, she was also more intelligent
and more strong-willed than her husband, King
Menelaos of Sparta. She ran away with her lover,
Paris, who took her to Troy. Menelaos had to prove
his manliness and get Helen back, otherwise people
would not respect him. So, with his powerful brother,
King Agamemnon of Mycenae, he organized a great
army and fleet to attack Troy.

Agamemnon and Achilles
For 10 years the forces of the two brothers besieged
Troy. The *Iliad* tells how Agamemnon made the
mistake of insulting his best warrior, Achilles, by
taking away his lover, Briseis. Achilles then refused
to fight. As a result, the Trojans, led by Prince Hektor,
did terrible damage to the besiegers until they killed
Achilles' close friend, Patroklos.

   This so enraged Achilles that he returned to the
fight, killed Hektor, tied his body to a chariot, and
then drove in triumph around the walls of Troy.
He was complete master of the field. None of the
Trojans dared to try and stop him. Achilles only
returned the body after Hektor's father begged
him to allow a proper funeral to take place.

▶ Beginning some 1,500
years after the era of ancient
Greece, European artists used
ancient Greek myths and
legends as subject matter for
their paintings. This artist is
imagining the Trojans fleeing
from their city after it has
been set on fire by the
Greeks. Notice the Corinthian
columns in the foreground
and the Ionic ones in the
background (see page 77).

◀ A picture of the famous
Trojan horse on a pot made
c.675 B.C.E. Men inside the
horse are handing weapons
to their comrades. Notice
their long hair and the
wheels of the horse.

▶ This detail from a painting
shows the wooden horse
being dragged into Troy.
The Greeks came out of
the horse at night, and the
city was taken. The story of
the wooden horse, which is
mentioned in Homer's poem
the *Odyssey*, may reflect
some tradition of an early
siege engine.

The wooden horse ends the siege

During the last part of the siege, which is not described in the *Iliad*, Achilles was killed by an arrow in his heel—the only part of his body that was not magically protected. Troy was then captured, but by means of a trick.

The attackers pretended to go home, but they left behind a large model horse made of wood. Curious, the Trojans dragged it into their city, only to discover too late that it was full of enemy soldiers. The gates were opened and Agamemnon's army poured into the city. Among those captured was Queen Helen.

How would Menelaos punish Helen for humiliating him, and for causing a war in which so many Greeks and Trojans had died? The Greeks said that Menelaos drew his sword, then dropped it—won over by the beauty of his wife's bosom. Helen became his queen again. Gracefully, she said she was sorry for the trouble she had caused!

Aristocrats and Poets

AFTER THE DARK AGE, FROM THE EIGHTH century B.C.E. onward, Greek history is colorful again. Greece was divided into many little independent communities. Most were ruled by their own small group of wealthy men. These men owned the best land. When they died, their sons ruled after them. Such people are known today as aristocrats. The Greeks had many names for them, including "the best" (*aristoi* in Greek), "the land sharers," and "the horse-breeders."

Wealth and horses

The horse was the symbol of an aristocrat's power and wealth, and an aristocratic child was often given a "horsey" name, the Greek for horse being *hippos*. For example, the father of Perikles was the wealthy Xanthippos ("yellow horse"). The father of Alexander the Great was King Philippos (Philip—"horse-lover"). Only the rich could afford good warhorses. A young aristocrat showed off his horse by riding in religious processions. Later, he could enjoy the rich man's sport of horse- and chariot-racing. After his death, his horses were again displayed—in the procession at his funeral.

Wine and poetry

The aristocrats of early Greece were famous for their wine-drinking. To get very drunk was a sign of wealth. Poor people perhaps could not afford much wine. They certainly could not afford to lose a day of work because of a hangover.

A drinking party for the rich was known as a *symposion*. Pretty young slave women—*hetairai*—often entertained, and many a symposion ended in an orgy. But other party guests behaved more thoughtfully. They were proud of their superior education, and a favorite party game was to compete in making up poetry on the spot.

▶ Places of importance in the age of the aristocrats. The poet Hesiod lived in the village of Askra and wrote that it was "hard in summer, bad in winter and never any good." The later poet Pindar, in contrast with Hesiod's bad feelings, wrote gushing praise of aristocrats and their lands. These and other major poets are listed below the map under their home cities.

◀ A poet sings his verses to a party of aristocrats, accompanying himself on the lyre. The guests drink from hand-painted pottery. They are all men, and a favorite theme of the poetry they would hear was the manly pursuit of war and deeds of battle.

Many of the poets who helped compose the *Iliad* and the *Odyssey* may have sung at parties like this. The two poems were certainly meant to please the rich. They usually show aristocratic characters as noble and heroic, while the character Thersites, who criticizes aristocrats, is described in the *Iliad* as ugly and ridiculous.

▶ This huge vase from the early sixth century B.C.E. shows activities favored by aristocrats, including a boar hunt. Horses are seen here galloping in a chariot race as well as walking in a solemn procession.

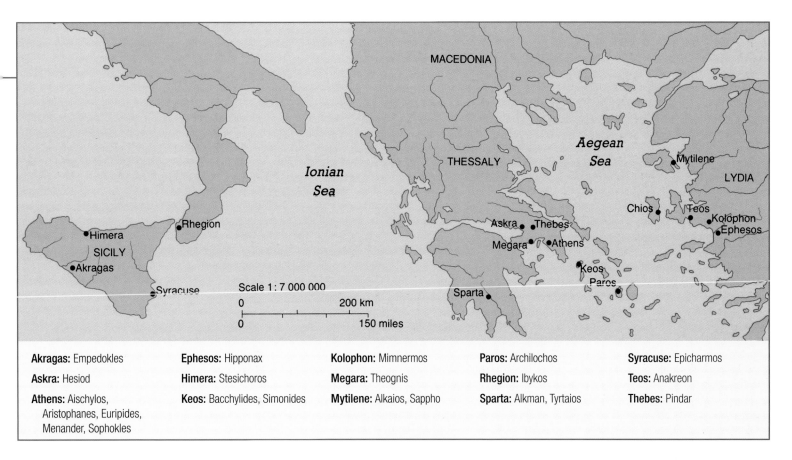

Akragas: Empedokles	**Ephesos:** Hipponax	**Kolophon:** Mimnermos	**Paros:** Archilochos	**Syracuse:** Epicharmos
Askra: Hesiod	**Himera:** Stesichoros	**Megara:** Theognis	**Rhegion:** Ibykos	**Teos:** Anakreon
Athens: Aischylos, Aristophanes, Euripides, Menander, Sophokles	**Keos:** Bacchylides, Simonides	**Mytilene:** Alkaios, Sappho	**Sparta:** Alkman, Tyrtaios	**Thebes:** Pindar

Professional poets also entertained the aristocrats. Skilled poetic flatterers—for example, Pindar of Thebes in the later classical period—made up fine verse in honor of the wealthy men who they hoped would reward them. One form of flattery was to praise the ancestors of a rich man and to suggest that they were connected with the gods.

Power of the aristocrats

The wealth enjoyed by the aristocrats was produced mainly by poor farmers, craftworkers, and slaves. Many, like the poet Hesiod in the eighth century B.C.E., resented the aristocracy. Hesiod claimed that when a rich man had a legal quarrel with a poor man, the rich man would often win by giving a bribe to the judge.

In the seventh century B.C.E., the power of the very rich declined. A new form of fighting—hoplite warfare—had been discovered (see pages 30–31). Now battles were decided by heavily armed footsoldiers, fighting in lines that bristled with spears and were protected by a wall of shields. Hoplites in close formation could defeat the cavalry of the aristocrats. In many cities, prosperous—but not aristocratic—men purchased their own military equipment and began to stand up to the aristocrats. A dictator, a *tyrannos*, often took control and crushed the aristocrats by taking their land. In the seventh and sixth centuries B.C.E. many important city-states, including Corinth, Athens, and Miletos, were ruled by tyrants. Sparta never had a tyranny.

Colonization

LIGURIA

Spina ○

Nikaia ■

Massalia ■

Emporion ■

Corsica

Alalia ■

Gravisca ○

Neap■

Poseidonia ▲

Sardinia

Sy

Hemeroskopeion ■

Mediterranean Sea

Sicily Himera Rheg

Selinus ● Naxos

Catana ■

Akragas ●

Syracuse ●

Scale 1 : 10 000 000

0   300 km

0   200 miles

THE GREEK COLONIES LAY SCATTERED from Asia Minor and the Black Sea coasts in the east as far as Italy, Sicily, and southern Spain in the west. There were also a few settlements on the coast of North Africa. However, the colonies never formed a great empire. The settlers usually stayed near the coast because Greeks felt uneasy if they were far from the sea. They traded with their non-Greek neighbors by land, and with each other by sea (see pages 38–39).

The colonists probably did not set out with thoughts of conquering a vast area. They went mainly in order to survive, although sometimes they were attracted by the profits to be made. Around 750 B.C.E. the poet Hesiod told of his own father, who had crossed the sea in search of a new home to escape "from wretched poverty." In the mountainous land of Greece little food could be produced—"bright-eyed hunger," in Hesiod's phrase, was a constant threat for many.

A story was told of the little island of Thera, where poverty forced some of the inhabitants to sail for Africa in the hope of founding a colony. When the first attempt failed and the men returned to Thera, their own people refused to have them back. They threw stones at their ships and would not let them land.

Trying to found a colony was dangerous. Firstly, there was the long sea voyage. Then there was a risk that non-Greeks who lived near the new colony would think it a threat and would attack it. In the 460s B.C.E., Athenians and other Greeks sent a large force (of about 10,000 men) to create a colony north of the Aegean Sea. Their venture was destroyed by local non-Greeks.

TRIPOLITANIA

The spread of Greek settlements

Colonization went in waves. After the fall of Mycenae, mainland Greeks moved east to settle in western Asia Minor and its offshore islands. From the eighth to the sixth centuries B.C.E. there was a movement north and west. Miletos in Asia Minor, itself a colony, founded scores of little colonies around the Black Sea. Corinth founded Kerkyra (Corfu) and Syracuse in the west. So many Greek colonies were founded in Sicily and southern Italy that the area is sometimes called Magna Graecia, which translates as "Great Greece."

■ Greek homeland, 11th–10th centuries B.C.E

Greek colony

● 11th–10th centuries

● 9th century

● 8th century

● 7th century

● 6th century

● 5th century

● Dorian

■ Ionian

✳ Aeolian

▼ Achaian

▲ Achaian/Troizenian

◆ East Greek

+ Athenian

○ Greek trading post

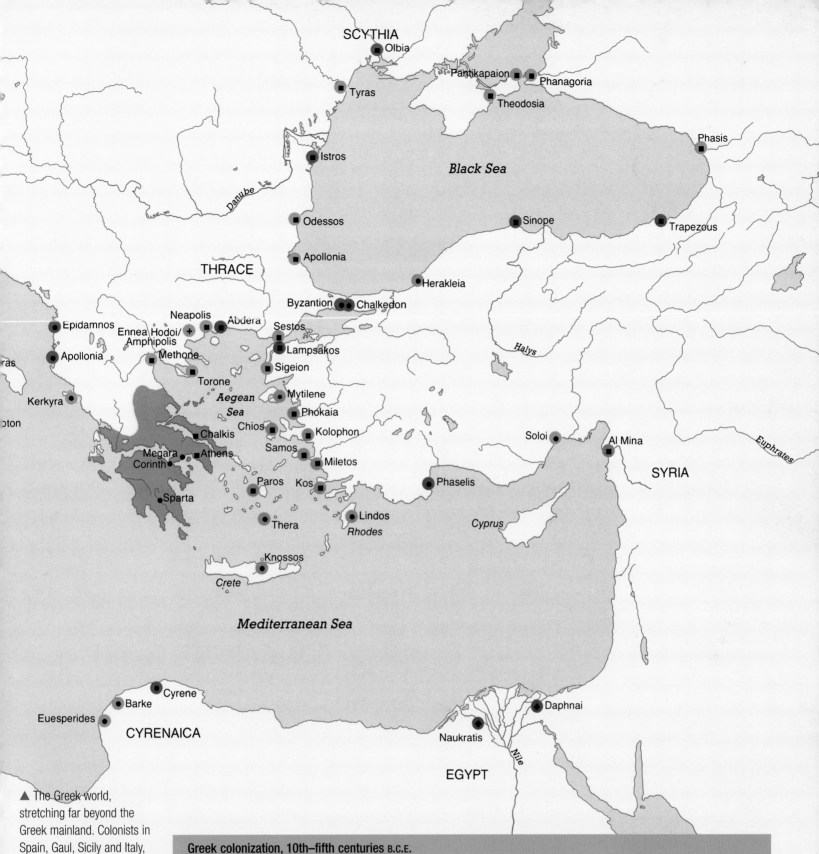

▲ The Greek world, stretching far beyond the Greek mainland. Colonists in Spain, Gaul, Sicily and Italy, Africa, Asia Minor, and the Black Sea coasts were all accepted as fully Greek, able to compete in the Olympic Games. Some of today's cities began as Greek colonies: Istanbul (Byzantion), Syracuse, Marseille (Massalia), Nice (Nikaia), and Naples (Neapolis).

Greek colonization, 10th–fifth centuries B.C.E.

c.1050–950 Colonization of western Asia Minor from mainland Greece.

Late eighth century Early Greek colonies in the west. Naxos, Syracuse, Catana in Sicily, and Sybaris, Taras, and Croton in southern Italy. Colonies multiply, dominating the coasts of the area.

Mid-seventh century Megara founds Byzantion, well placed to control the entrance to the Black Sea.

c.630 Thera founds Cyrene in North Africa.

Mid-seventh–early sixth century Miletos rings the Black Sea with its colonies.

Late seventh century Naukratis founded: a Greek trading post in Egypt.

c.600 Phokaia (city-state in western Asia Minor) founds Massalia in southern Gaul.

c.510 Sybaris destroyed by Croton.

Mid-460s Disastrous attempt of Athenians and others to found large colony at Ennea Hodoi near coast of northern Aegean.

440s–430s Athenians establish colonies north of the Aegean.

Magna Graecia and the Tyrants

GREEK COLONISTS IN MAGNA GRAECIA (present-day Sicily and southern Italy) developed power and wealth that were envied by many in the Greek homeland.

The legendary city of Sybaris

Other Greeks joked about the splendor and luxury that was said to characterize Sybaris. They claimed the Sybarites had beds made of rose petals, and that noisy crafts, such as carpentry, were banned so the citizens could sleep peacefully in the daytime after their nights at drunken parties.

Such tales, although exaggerated, reflected the wealth that visitors could see in western Greek cities. Sybaris was utterly destroyed in war in the late sixth century, but remains of its colony Poseidonia (Paestum) can still be seen.

Gelon, tyrant of Sicily

Akragas also has the remains of splendid buildings. Like other Sicilian towns around 500 B.C.E., Akragas was ruled by an autocrat, a *tyrannos*. The most famous of these rulers was Gelon, tyrant of Gela. Admiring Syracuse with its large natural harbor, Gelon made it his capital. To this magnificent site, he moved many of the people of Gela and also the wealthy classes from Kamarina and Megara.

Carthage, a non-Greek state in North Africa, felt threatened by the new power of Gelon and his allies and invaded Sicily with an huge force. Gelon's army destroyed the Carthaginian army in 480 B.C.E. at Himera. Carthaginians taken prisoner after the battle helped build the great temples of Akragas.

In Sicily, Gelon favored aristocrats and sold many poor citizens into slavery. In the Greek homeland,

▼ The tyrannies in the Greek homeland and Magna Graecia, from the seventh to the fifth centuries B.C.E. The age of the tyrants saw much prosperity, with fine buildings and, in Athens and Corinth, magnificent pottery. With many enemies among their own citizens, tyrants of different cities cooperated with each other rather than making war on one another.

◄ Colonies in Sicily. In Sicily the Greek cities were mainly in the east—the side that colonists sailing from the homeland would approach first. Syracuse sucked in people and power from neighboring cities, and even conquered a great Athenian force in 413 B.C.E.

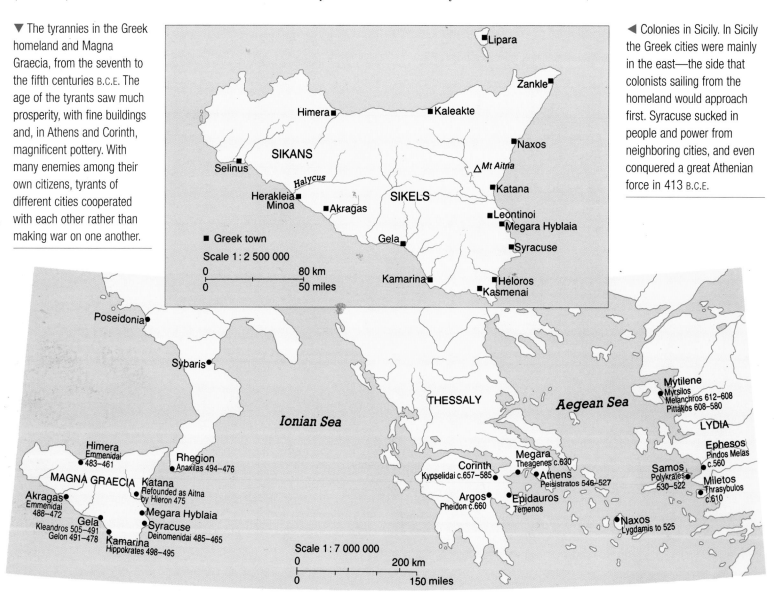

▶ This vase was made at Athens in the age of tyranny, when a famous fountain was constructed in the city. It shows women filling pitchers with water from the fountain.

▼ Wonderful temples survive in Poseidonia (Paestum), a colony of Sybaris, itself a colony in southern Italy. This temple dates from the mid-fifth century B.C.E., 50 years after the fall of Sybaris itself. Refugee families from Sybaris may have helped build it.

however, tyrants were very different. There they were often antiaristocratic and were champions of the hoplites, who were footsoldiers. Hoplites were prosperous men who could afford their own expensive military equipment (see pages 17 and 30–31), although compared with the aristocrats they were not rich.

Kypselos, the first tyrant of Corinth, crushed the aristocracy of his city. Peisistratos, tyrant of Athens, drove many Athenian aristocrats into exile and won a reputation as a humane and fair-minded ruler. Pittakos, tyrant of Mytilene, was especially hard on the notorious failing of aristocrats—drunkenness. Anyone who committed a crime when drunk was given a double penalty: one for the crime and one for getting drunk in the first place.

The Warlike Spartans

I N THE SOUTHERN PELOPONNESE WAS A small, strange, and frightening community—Sparta. Its power was to grow until it dominated most of Greece. Early in their history the Spartans had conquered the fertile land of Lakonia. Later, perhaps in the mid-seventh century B.C.E., they finally conquered the Messenians to the west.

Slaves in Sparta—the helots

The defeated Greek people in the regions of Lakonia and Messenia became known as "helots." They were forced to work for the Spartans. The men had to labor on the land to produce food, while the women had to make clothes.

The helots were treated like slaves. They hated the Spartans. It was even said that the helots would gladly eat the Spartans raw. The Spartans knew this.

Because there were far more helots than Spartans, Sparta was anxious to prevent the helots from rising up in revolt. So the wealthy men of Sparta gave up their relaxed drinking parties and expensive tastes.

► This handsome vessel was made by a Spartan craftsman in the sixth century B.C.E., before Sparta turned its back on art and luxuries. It is huge—66 in (168 cm) high, and was probably used for mixing wine and water. Around the neck, molded in bronze, is a procession of war chariots and hoplites. The vessel was found in France.

▼ The Peloponnese with Lakonia, Sparta's homeland. In the mid-sixth century B.C.E. Sparta dominated most of the Peloponnese. By the end of the century the Spartans were ready to strike out into central Greece—against Athens.

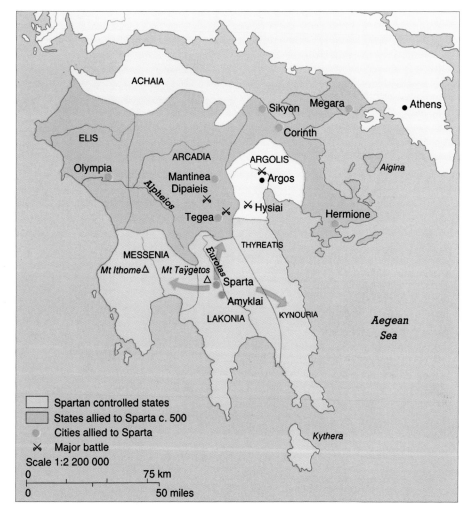

Spartan controlled states
States allied to Sparta c. 500
● Cities allied to Sparta
✗ Major battle
Scale 1:2 200 000
0 — 75 km
0 — 50 miles

Instead, Spartans began to live the hard, disciplined life of soldiers, constantly ready to fight helots.

The Spartan army

By day the Spartans practiced for war. Their ranks of hoplites (infantry) learned complicated maneuvers, involving set moves that resemble those in football today. The purpose was to deceive and surprise enemies on the battlefield, so outsiders were forbidden to watch these exercises.

But they were allowed to see the harsh exercise that made young Spartans strong and brave. This was one of the means by which Sparta cleverly scared its enemies. Another was that Spartan soldiers grew their hair long, to make them look bigger and fiercer.

There were also many horsemen. As they patrolled their large territory on horseback, they would have appeared powerful and frightening to the helots, who went on foot.

At night the Spartans learned to move without the use of torches. They also knew the importance of attacking when the enemy was weakest, and they often caught their opponents sleepy and confused. Helots were probably forbidden to go out at night, in order to stop them from plotting secretly against the Spartans. Groups of young Spartans crept about in the dark with knives and would kill any helots they found out of doors.

▶ Landscape—mountains to the east, north, and west, and sea to the south—defended Sparta. Mount Taÿgetos, right, separates Lakonia from Messenia. In the foreground is the fertile plain of Sparta.

▼ Spartan hoplites gaze into enemy territory. Before invading, their commander will check whether or not the gods approve of the venture. He will sacrifice a goat then examine its guts for "good" or "bad" signs.

Control over neighboring states

If an enemy state from the north were to invade Spartan territory, the helots could revolt by joining the invaders. So Sparta used its army to set up pro-Spartan governments in the central and northern Peloponnese. These governments would defend the Spartans, not attack them. The government of Tegea in the mid-sixth century B.C.E. promised not to help helots who escaped from Spartan control. The powerful state of Argos remained an enemy.

In 494 B.C.E. a Spartan king named Kleomenes used a trick to defeat an army from Argos. He knew that the enemy could hear the orders that were shouted to his own army. So, secretly telling his men to be ready for battle, he let his crier shout out that it was time for a meal. The enemy heard this and relaxed. They began to eat, too. Kleomenes's men attacked and won the day.

In 464 B.C.E. the helots began a revolt that lasted for nine years. The helots of Messenia finally won their freedom in 369 B.C.E.

Athens and Democracy

I N PREHISTORIC TIMES ATTICA WAS A REGION that contained many tiny independent villages. Much later, in the great days of Athens, stories were told of the legendary King Theseus who, it was said, had united all the villages into one state. Its capital was Athens. Its citizens, most of whom were still country-dwellers, were all Athenians.

The Akropolis

The focus of the unified state was the great rock of Athens —the Akropolis ("high city"). From the rock there were splendid views over land and sea. But the Athenians did not value the views for the same reason that tourists do today. They needed the views to tell them when an enemy was approaching.

A fortress was built on the Akropolis. There families could shelter from an enemy. And if the enemy tried to climb—slowly—the steep sides of the rock, they would make an easy target for arrows, and for spears, stones, and boulders hurled by the Athenians from above.

Athens in the early historical period, sixth–fifth centuries B.C.E.

Late 590s A bitter quarrel between rich and poor of Athens is solved. Spared a civil war, Athens has the strength to expand. Not long afterward, Athenians capture the island of Salamis from neighboring Megara (see map). Peisistratos commands the victorious forces.

c.546 At the third attempt Peisistratos manages to make himself sole ruler ("tyrant") of Athens. Under the tyranny fine buildings and beautiful painted pottery are made.

c.510 The tyranny ends in blood. Hippias, Peisistratos's son, who killed many citizens, is thrown out.

508–507 Beginnings of a new revolutionary style of government —*demokratia*, the rule of the people.

Late 480s A big new supply of silver is found in Athens' mines at Laureion. The Athenians decide to spend it on building a large fleet of warships. This is just in time because . . .

480–479 . . . Persia invades Greece with an enormous fleet and army (see pages 26–27). Although defeated, the Persians destroy much of Athens.

479 onward Athenians return and hurriedly build a great defensive wall around their city, and fortify a new port. It will become the most famous in the Mediterranean—Peiraieus.

▼ Socrates made himself unpopular by asking difficult questions such as "What is true justice?" and "What does 'knowledge' mean?" People could not answer and were embarrassed. Condemned to death for "corrupting the young" and "introducing new gods," Socrates refused to escape and died by drinking poison in 399 B.C.E.

◄ Attica became wealthy from producing olive oil. Silver from mines at Laureion enriched Athens and made its coins. By conquering the great islands of Salamis (early sixth century B.C.E.) and Aigina (mid-fifth century), Athens made safe its profitable seaborne trade into Phaleron and Peiraieus.

[Map of Attica region]

● Thebes

BOIOTIA

● Tanagra

EUBOIA

Gulf of Euripos

Asopos

OROPOS

● Plataia

◆ Panakton

◆ Oinoe

Dekeleia ◆

Charadra

● Marathon

◆ Leipsydrion

Gulf of Corinth

Probalinthos ●

● Pagai

ATTICA

MEGARID

Eleusis ◆

Kephisos

● Megara

CORINTH

Nisaia ●

Salamis ●

● Athens

Salamis

Peiraieus ●

● Phaleron

Saronic Gulf

● Brauron

● Anagyrous

● Kephale

● Aigina
Aigina

Anaphlystos ●

Laureion ●

● Sounion

Legend:
- ● Village
- ● Town
- ◆ Fort
- —·—·— State boundary
- – – – Sacred Way
- ▨ Attica in 6th century
- ☐ Area controlled by Athens

Scale 1 : 600 000
0 _____ 15 km
0 _____ 10 miles

▲ *Ostraka*, bits of pot, with the names of important Athenian politicians: Aristeides, Kimon, and Themistokles.

▼ When rival politicians put forward conflicting plans, Athenians would sometimes vote with pieces of pottery to decide which politicians to banish. The loser was ostracized—sent into exile for 10 years. Broken pots were cheap and plentiful.

◄ Disks such as these were used by jurymen voting in the law courts. Each juryman was given two—one solid and one with a hole in the middle. One meant "not guilty," the other "guilty." As each juryman came to the pot into which he dropped his disk, he kept his thumb over the middle of it. That way onlookers could not tell how he was voting.

▲ Aristotle came to Athens from a tiny country town to study and meet clever people. He wrote about physics, biology, politics, and religion.

▲ Thucydides, a rich Athenian, became a general but was exiled. He wrote a history of war between Athens and Sparta.

The beginning of "people-power"

In every Greek state, so Aristotle tells us, there were a few rich people and a large number of the poor. Rich and poor usually plotted against each other. Sometimes they even fought, in a civil war. Greeks called this quarreling *stasis*. Many states were weakened by it. One reason why Athens and Sparta became so powerful is that they both managed to avoid much *stasis*.

Rich Spartan landowners dealt with the problem harshly. They treated their poor, the helots, like slaves and terrified them into obedience. But Athens was far gentler. There the poor had great power as well as freedom. Poor citizens controlled the chief decision-making bodies, the assembly and the law courts. This was *demokratia*. *Demos*, means "the ordinary people," and *kratos* means "power." So *demokratia* literally meant "people-power." It was largely an Athenian invention.

Why did the rich put up with "people-power"? Rich men, who could afford the best education and learned public speaking, had the most confidence. They could often persuade the crowds of ordinary people. There were many teachers of the art of public speaking, and some became famous for their skill in producing clever and convincing arguments.

Shall we go to war? What taxes shall we pay? Shall we spend our city's money on warships or on new buildings? Big questions such as these were decided by the votes of thousands of ordinary citizens in the assembly. It usually met on a hillside near the Akropolis. All male citizens, regardless of their wealth, had one vote each.

War Against Persia

TO THE EAST OF THE GREEK WORLD LAY a vast enemy power—Persia. Its empire stretched from the shores of the Aegean Sea to India, and from Russia as far as Egypt. Its wealth and numbers of people were far greater than those of the neighboring Greeks.

Many Greeks in Asia Minor belonged for years to the Persian Empire. In the 490s B.C.E. some of them—Ionians led by the city of Miletos—dared to rebel against Persian power. From across the Aegean a force of Athenians came to help them. The rebels burned Sardis, the base of the local Persian governor, but in 494 B.C.E. the rebellion was crushed. As punishment, the Persians wrecked Miletos. Milesian boys were mutilated. The prettiest girls were dragged away to serve the Great King of Persia, Darius.

The battle of Marathon

King Darius began to make plans to punish Athens. In 490 B.C.E. his Persian invasion force crossed the Aegean Sea, landing troops on the plain of

▶ The battlefield of Thermopylai. The land takes the form of a narrow pass, or strip, between the Gulf of Euboia and the Pindos Mountains. It forms a gateway to central Greece. Greek forces at first defended the pass successfully, but they were eventually overcome by the Persians.

▼ Persian expeditions. The invaders of 490 B.C.E. sailed to Marathon. In 480 B.C.E. Xerxes' far larger force, (land army and fleet) progressed along the coasts of Asia Minor and mainland Greece. To cross the Hellespont they made a bridge of boats.

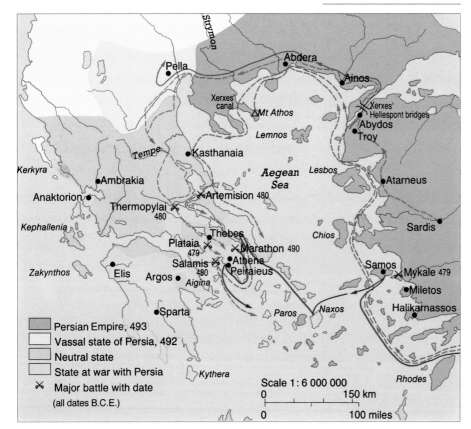

Persian Empire, 493
Vassal state of Persia, 492
Neutral state
State at war with Persia
✕ Major battle with date
(all dates B.C.E.)

Scale 1 : 6 000 000
0   150 km
0   100 miles

----▶ Route of Persian fleet under Mardonios, 492
——▶ Route of Persian army under Darius, 492
——▶ Route of Persian fleet under Datis, 490
----▶ Route of Persian fleet under Xerxes, 480
----▶ Route of Persian army under Xerxes, 480

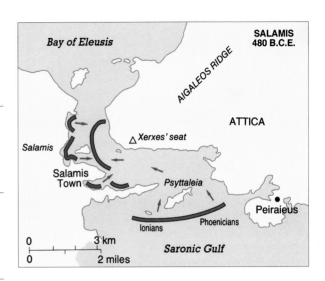

◀ A Greek with a metal helmet fights a lightly clad Persian soldier. Greeks often wore shinguards (greaves) and breastplates.

▶ The battle of Salamis, with the Persian fleet about to sail into the narrows where the Greeks are waiting.

▼ The Athenians come down from the hills to attack the Persians who have invaded from the sea.

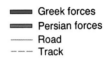
- ▬ Greek forces
- ▬ Persian forces
- — Road
- --- Track

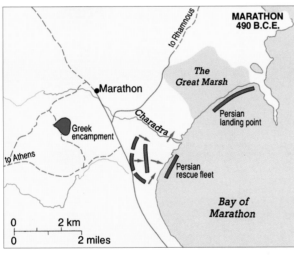

Marathon, near Athens. In the battle that followed, however, the Athenians showed that heavily armed Greek hoplites were superior to the light-armed Persians. Defeated, the invaders were chased back to their ships. Later, a tale was told of a runner who brought the news of victory from Marathon to Athens. This was the first Marathon run, and the distance was a little less than 30 miles (48 km).

The great invasion of 480 B.C.E.

Twice humiliated by Athens, the Persians, led by Darius's son King Xerxes, organized an invasion that would finally settle matters. The Greeks sent spies but they were caught. They were later set free to take home a terrifying message: Xerxes' new force was so large it was hard to imagine.

The Greek historian Herodotos calculated that it contained more than 5 million men. The chief Greek powers, Sparta and Athens, had fewer than 50,000 warriors. They realized that their greatest danger lay in being cut off from supplies and unable to maneuver. A force that is surrounded is nearly always defeated. So the Greeks, under Spartan control, decided to fight in narrow places where the Persians would be blocked.

First the Greeks defended the narrow pass at Thermopylai with an army, and the nearby channel of Artemision with a fleet—to prevent Persian ships from landing troops in the army's rear and surrounding it. But, hoping to be rewarded, a treacherous Greek showed the Persians a mountain track which enabled them to trap 300 Spartans. The betrayed Spartans died fighting.

Xerxes' men poured through the pass and went on to capture Athens. But the city they found was by now largely empty. Athens' warriors were with the Greek fleet in a nearby channel at Salamis. What probably happened next was that a secret message went to Xerxes: "the Greeks are quarreling—attack at Salamis and you will win easily." Xerxes sent in his fleet—but it was a trap. Heavy Greek ships crashed into the lighter Persian vessels. Shipwrecked Persian sailors were stabbed in the water like fish.

The victory at Salamis proved to be crucial for the Greeks. Xerxes and much of his force went back to Asia. In 479 B.C.E. the remaining Persian army was crushed at Plataia. The great invasion was over. The Greeks had finally won.

The Trireme—Greek Warship

ATHENS CONTROLLED ITS EXTENSIVE EMPIRE (see page 32) by the use of warships. In ancient times, as today, many of the Greeks lived on the islands of the Aegean. By ruling the sea, Athens could decide which goods and which troops went to and from these islands. In addition, warships were needed to protect Athens' own merchant vessels as they brought food and luxuries to the Athenian port of Peiraieus.

The warship which Athens used to such good effect was the trireme. A trireme was a wooden galley powered in battle by up to 170 oarsmen arranged in three tiers. At the height of its power Athens had about 300 triremes in service. A trireme did not carry artillery, and on board there were at most 30 marines armed and ready for hand-to-hand fighting. How then did triremes win a battle?

How the triremes fought a battle

Built into the bow of every vessel, below the waterline, was a long wooden ram sheathed in bronze. Each trireme aimed to sink enemy warships by crashing head-on into the weakest part of an enemy ship—namely, its side.

▼ Triremes in battle. There was only a handful of armed men on deck. Most of the casualties happened when triremes, shattered by the rams of the enemy, spilled their men into the water. There they either drowned, or were speared "like tuna fish" by enemy marines.

► How did the three banks of rowers sit, and how did they manage to pull their oars together? It has taken scholars many decades to work this out and to create the reconstruction that now sails the Aegean. On an ancient trireme, a piper played so that the rowers moved in time and did not tangle their oars.

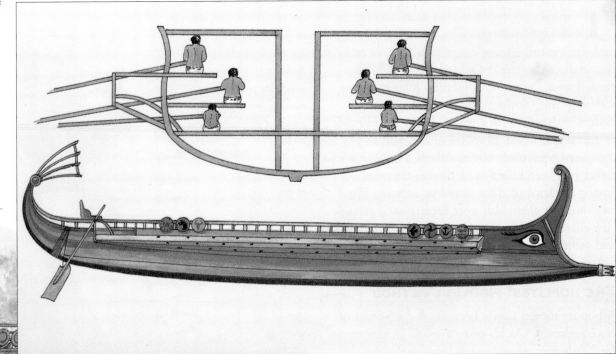

Rammed amidships by a trireme at speed, a vessel's timbers would shatter and it would then sink. It was therefore the job of a ship's crew to make sure that their trireme was not caught with its side exposed to attack. Victory depended on being able to maneuver quickly. Athenian rowers, and especially their helmsmen, made themselves expert at this through long practice.

The Athenians' tactical mastery

The enemies of Athens in the mid-fifth century B.C.E. recognized the superiority of the Athenian naval skills and usually did not attempt to challenge with triremes of their own.

In 429 B.C.E. a little Athenian fleet in the Corinthian Gulf was faced with a far larger group of enemy Peloponnesian warships. So as not to be outmaneuvered and rammed amidships, the Peloponnesian ships formed a circle, with their bows outward like the spokes of a wheel. But the Athenian commander, Phormion, made his ships circle around and around the enemy, whose ships nervously backed closer together.

Then a wind sprang up, as Phormion had expected. The enemy were by now tightly bunched and the wind blew them into confusion, the oars and hulls of different vessels becoming entangled and helpless. Phormion's ships then charged into them and won a decisive victory.

Hoplites—Greek Fighters

T HE GREEK HOPLITE WAS THE MOST FEARED soldier of his day in the lands around the eastern Mediterranean. From the seventh to the mid-fourth centuries B.C.E., no foreign force knew how to match the hoplite.

Hoplites were men who carried *hopla* ("arms"). These included a long spear for stabbing (not for throwing), a short sword, a helmet, and—especially important—a round heavy shield made of metal and wood. Hoplites usually had to pay for their own equipment, but in Athens a hoplite whose father had been killed in battle was rewarded by having his arms paid for at public expense. The wealthiest of them also wore breastplates, greaves (leg guards), and strips of metal to protect their thighs and groin. Poorer men may have fought almost naked except for their shields.

The hoplites' fighting method

A hoplite moved slowly because of the weight of his equipment. On his own he made an easy target for quick-moving opponents, such as cavalry, archers, and slingers. One Greek writer said that hoplites, if disorganized, were "useless." Why, then, did they prove so terrifying?

The answer is that hoplites fought in a close formation, known as a phalanx. It consisted of several lines of men, shoulder to shoulder. Protected by an unbroken line of shields, the phalanx bristled with spears. The spears of the hoplites were much like the bristles of a porcupine. On its own a spear, like a bristle, could be dealt with. But massed together, the sharp points were formidable. Even armed cavalrymen would not charge an unbroken line of hoplites, for fear that each horse and rider would be skewered by several spears at once.

Importance of shield and helmet

When opposing lines of hoplites met in battle, each tried to break through the other's phalanx. Once that was done, the victorious hoplites rushed through the gap for the easier job of attacking the opponents in their undefended flanks and rear. To prevent this, it was vital that a line of shields remained unbroken. So for extra strength each shield was supported in two ways at once. The hoplite's arm went through a loop behind the center of the shield, and his hand gripped a handle just behind the rim. But the hoplite had to be able to see over the top of his shield, making his head and neck the chief targets for enemy spears. That is why helmets were so important.

▶ When opposing hoplites met face to face, killing was done by jabbing spears downward at the face and throat. Shown here are various types of helmet, designed at different periods, but all meant to protect as much as possible of this vulnerable area of the body.

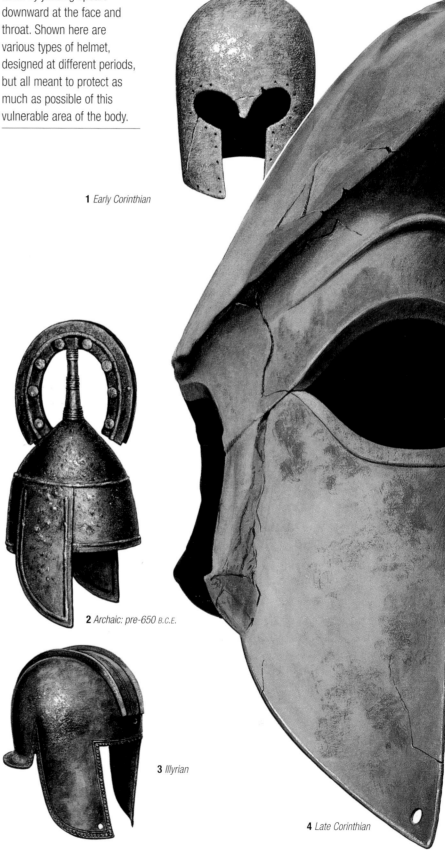

1 *Early Corinthian*

2 *Archaic: pre-650 B.C.E.*

3 *Illyrian*

4 *Late Corinthian*

► A hoplite was armed not only to kill others and protect himself, but also to radiate confidence and frighten the enemy. The high crest of his helmet made him appear taller and stronger than he really was.

Wars of the Athenian Empire

AFTER THE DEFEATS AT SALAMIS AND Plataia, the Persians fled back to Asia. The Greeks were relieved, but they could not relax—the Persians might invade later. They decided to attack now, while the enemy was weak. Salamis had shown that the fleet of Athens was the best in Greece, and a fleet was needed for attacking the long, Persian-controlled coasts. Also, Athens was keen to go on fighting. (The Spartans wanted to go home to guard their helots.) So eastern Greeks turned for leadership to Athens.

From 477 B.C.E. Athens' allies put money into a treasury on the island of Delos in order to pay for the continuing war against Persia. But Athens took more and more control over how the money was spent, and eventually all the money was taken to Athens. Like it or not, the allies had to go on paying. The Delian League had turned into an Athenian empire. The allies' money was used to create lovely buildings, which can still be seen (pages 74–77). But the Athenians had money to spare for war against other Greeks.

War against Sparta

The Spartans had become afraid. Would Athens one day use its great power against them? Sparta watched Athens like a tomcat about to fight. It waited patiently for a sign of weakness to exploit, then sprang. For 60 years from 465 B.C.E., every time Athens showed any weakness Sparta planned a new attack. These bursts of fighting between Athens and Sparta are called the Peloponnesian Wars.

In the early 450s B.C.E. many Athenian troops were far away in Egypt, fighting the Persians. Sparta struck, defeating the Athenians at the battle of Tanagra, but failing to capture Athens itself. In 431 B.C.E. Athens was again vulnerable, for many of its allies were in revolt. Sparta struck once more, invading Attica and burning crops. From their city walls Athenians watched in rage. Their homes and farms were on fire. They longed to go out and fight, but that was just what the Spartans wanted. Spartan hoplites were likely to win, since Athens' power lay in its navy. Intelligently led by Perikles, Athens did not face Sparta in a big land battle. Instead, Athens' navy took its revenge by raiding the Peloponnese.

Sparta allies with Persia

In 413 B.C.E. Athens lost more than half its ships in a disastrous attempt to capture Sicily. Seeing Athens' greatest weakness, Sparta made an alliance with Persia and, using Persian money, built a fleet. In 405 B.C.E. Athens' seaborne grain supply was cut off. The news was passed from Peiraieus to Athens with screaming and wailing. The following year Athens was starved into surrender. Sparta did not destroy the city, as some of her allies would have liked, but Athens was rendered defenseless and her navy reduced to only 12 triremes. The empire was over.

▼ The areas controlled by Athens and Sparta in the late fifth century B.C.E. Sparta's land army dominated its neighboring states. Athens' warships ruled the islands and the remoter coastal cities. The fleet guarded Athens' grain supply, which came over the Black Sea and past Byzantion into the Aegean.

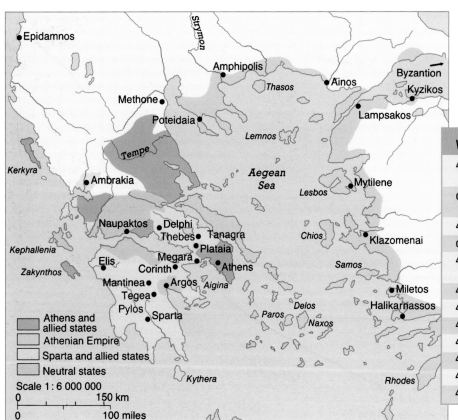

Athens and allied states
Athenian Empire
Sparta and allied states
Neutral states

Scale 1 : 6 000 000

0 ——— 150 km
0 ——— 100 miles

Wars of the Athenian Empire, 478–404 B.C.E.
478–477 Greek states join Athens in the new Delian League, to fight Persia.
c.469 The League crushes the Persian navy at Eurymedon in southeast Asia Minor.
465 Sparta first plans to attack Athens.
c.460–455 Athens' attempt to capture Egypt defeated.
458 or 457 Sparta beats Athens at Tanagra but gains little military advantage.
454–453 The League treasury is moved to Athens.
447 The treasury starts to be used to build the Parthenon.
431 Sparta starts the great Peloponnesian War.
425 Athens captures Spartans alive on Sphakteria.
413 Athens loses a huge fleet in Sicily.
405 The Spartan fleet cuts off Athens' supply of food.
404 Athenians, starving, surrender to Sparta.

◄ A hoplite, poised to strike (raised spear not shown) at an enemy.

► In 425 B.C.E. Athens put men ashore at Pylos. Sparta blundered by putting its own troops on the nearby island of Sphakteria, where Athenians captured them.

▼ A view from the north of the site of ancient Pylos, with Sphakteria in the background.

PYLOS AND SPHAKTERIA 425 B.C.E.

N

Spartan camp
Pylos
Athenian walls
prehistoric fort
Sphakteria
Ionian Sea
Bay of Navarino
Spartan camp
landing of Athenian fleet
Spartan outpost

0   1 km
0   1 mile

The Siege of Plataia

PLATAIA, A LITTLE TOWN IN BOIOTIA, WAS for a long time an ally of Athens. This spelled trouble for the Plataians, since not far from them was the large city of Thebes, which was usually an enemy of Athens (see map on page 32). In fact, Thebans thought it outrageous that Plataia should be allied to Athens. Plataia was part of Boiotia, and Boiotia was traditionally dominated by Thebes. Plataia would have to be crushed.

The first Theban attack

In 431 B.C.E. Thebes made a surprise attack on Plataia. A group of Thebans got into the town at night and tried to take over. But when the Plataians found out how few the invaders were, they decided to fight them. Secretly, and without going into the streets, the Plataians assembled ready to attack. They did this by burrowing their way from house to house, through the mud-brick walls (the layout of town houses made this easy—see page 90).

The Plataian attack was too much for the Thebans. While the men fought the invaders in the streets, some women climbed onto the roofs and pelted the Thebans with tiles and stones. The Thebans were either killed immediately or later, having first surrendered.

Thebes and Sparta strike again

After this humiliation and loss of life, Thebes hated the Plataians even more. Two years later, in 429 B.C.E., the Thebans tried again, with very different results. This time Thebes had Sparta's help, while Plataia had a little support from Athens. The Spartans, who wanted unhindered access into Attica from the Peloponnese, brought the full army of their alliance to capture Plataia—probably more than 10,000 men. Inside the town walls the defenders numbered less than one-twentieth of this: 400 Plataians and 80 Athenians. (There were also 110 women to prepare their food.)

▶ The Athenian writer Thucydides gives us so much detail about the siege of Plataia that we can roughly reconstruct it. Wall no. 1 in the picture is that finally built by the besiegers, which trapped many defenders inside. Below the defenders' main wall (no. 2) is the mouth of their secret tunnel, invisible to the attackers outside. Wall no. 3 is the Plataians' defense against the Thebans' earthwork—the mound—which the Thebans tried to build against the town wall and then use to invade the town.

How Plataia withstood the siege

The little army of defenders worked hard and smartly. Outside the town wall the besiegers began to build an earth mound. The plan was to build it as high as the wall so that the besiegers could walk up the mound onto the top of the wall, and use their superior numbers to capture the town. But secretly the Plataians built a tunnel under their wall and out under the mound. While the besiegers piled earth onto the mound, the defenders tunneled away beneath, bringing earth back inside the town. Not surprisingly, the mound made little progress!

The besiegers tried to use siege machines and battering rams. But the defenders threw ropes from the wall, lassoed the machines, dragged them up, and broke them. They snapped the battering rams by dropping great wooden beams on them.

In case the besiegers managed to finish their mound and climb up onto the wall, the defenders built a new stretch of wall, in a crescent shape, inside the wall that the mound was threatening. (The new wall is no. 3 in our picture.) If attackers from the mound captured a section of the main wall, they would then have to spend more months building another mound to capture this new wall.

The end of the two-year siege

The besiegers used fire against the town, throwing in bundles of burning brushwood. The defenders were saved by the wind direction. Finally the besiegers built a brick wall of their own right around the town (no. 1). A few men were enough to guard it. Some defenders escaped over this wall, using ladders on a dark night. The rest starved. They surrendered in 427 B.C.E., and all were killed.

Sparta gave the town to Thebes, and Thebes demolished it. Plataia was later rebuilt, only to be destroyed by Thebes in 373 B.C.E. King Philip of Macedon (see page 42) rebuilt the town again after his conquest of Greece in 338 B.C.E.

Greek Coinage

COINS FIRST APPEARED IN THE NON-GREEK kingdom of Lydia in Asia Minor shortly before 600 B.C.E. The Greeks quickly copied the idea. Independent Greek city-states, both large and small, issued their own coinage. As a result, there is a great variety of interesting and fine-looking coin types.

Why have coins at all? The first coins seem to have been too valuable for use in everyday trade. They may have been meant to pay large regular outgoings, such as the salaries of officials. However, coins of bronze—a cheap metal—later became commonplace and were used in daily shopping. (We hear of shoppers in Athens, for example, carrying coins like these in their mouths.)

Designed to prevent dishonesty

The marks on a coin were a guarantee, issued by the authorities of a city-state, of how much metal the coin contained. A distinctive design showed which city had issued the coin.

With coinage of gold and silver, there was a danger that people would secretly cut off small bits of the metal and collect them, before spending the coin itself. So by putting official marks, or a picture, on the back as well as on the front of each coin, the cities made sure that people could tell when a face of the coin had been shaved. A raised circle around the rim also made it obvious when someone had been shaving the edge.

Coins minted from c.600 to 170 B.C.E.

The captions refer first to the obverse (left) and then the reverse of the coins. Unless stated otherwise, the coins are of silver.

1 **Samos, c.600.** One of the earliest coins, made of electrum (an alloy of gold and silver).
2 **Miletos, c.570.** Of electrum, the obverse shows a lion.
3 **Aigina, c.560.** Obverse shows a turtle.
4 **Lydia, c.550.** Home of the first coinage.
5 **Corinth, c.520.** Pegasus, the mythical winged horse.
6 **Dikaia, c.520.** Showing Herakles' lion-skin cap.
7 **Sybaris, c.520.** From this rich, doomed city. The bull indicates wealth in cattle.
8 **Rhegion, c.390.** Lion's head and Apollo.
9 **Thourioi, c.390.** Thourioi was a colony founded by Athens on the former land of Sybaris. The coin shows the head of Athena and the bull of Sybaris (see no. 7).
10 **Aspendos, c.380.** Wrestlers and a slinger.
11 **Syracuse, c.485.** A racing chariot and the local nymph Arethousa ringed with dolphins.
12 **Ainos, c.465.** The god Hermes and a goat.
13 **Athens, c.440.** The goddess Athena, defender of Athens, and her owl.
14 **Mende, c.430.** Dionysos riding an ass, and a vine.
15 **Messana, c.430.** A mule-drawn racing chariot and a hare with the head of Pan below.

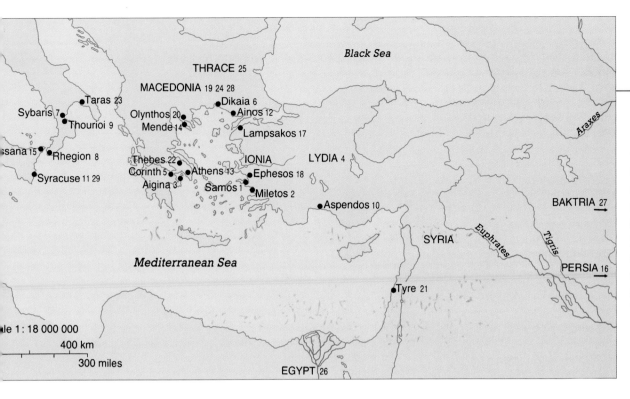

The map shows where the coins illustrated here were made. After the invention of coinage in Lydia, the idea spread to the Greeks of Asia Minor—to trading cities such as Aigina, Corinth, and Athens as well as to the wealthy cities of the west.

16 **Persia, fifth–fourth century.** Gold coin of Persian king with bow and arrows.

17 **Lampsakos, c.350.** Gold coin with Zeus and the winged horse Pegasus.

18 **Ephesos, c.350.** Bee, stag, and palm tree.

19 **Macedonia, mid-fourth century.** Gold coin with Zeus and chariot, commemorating Olympic victory.

20 **Olynthos, c.375.** Apollo and his lyre.

21 **Tyre, a non-Greek state, c.360.** The reverse shows Egyptian emblems.

22 **Thebes, mid-fourth century.** Hoplite shield and amphora.

23 **Taras, c.330.** Warrior and horse, and dolphin-rider. Taras, a colony in south Italy, often used these coins to hire mercenaries to ward off local non-Greek peoples.

24 **Macedonia, c.330.** A coin of Alexander the Great, showing him dressed as Herakles in a lion-skin cap. The other image is of Zeus. The silver for this coin may well have come from treasure captured from Persia.

25 **Thrace, c.300.** This coin was issued by one of Alexander's successors, Lysimachos, and shows Alexander as the god Ammon.

26 **Egypt, c.300.** A coin of Ptolemy, Alexander's former general who gained control of Egypt. It shows Ptolemy himself.

27 **Baktria, c.180.** One of the most easterly kingdoms to emerge from Alexander's empire.

28 **Macedonia's last king, Perseus, c.170.** He was defeated by Rome at Pydna in 168.

29 **Syracuse, third century.** The coin shows Philistis, wife of the ruler of Syracuse, Hieron II.

The coins numbered 1 to 29 show a progress from the simple, early markings around 600 B.C.E. (1–2) to the realistic portraits in the late, Hellenistic, period (24–29).

Some coins were meant to delight the eye. Look at the elaborate hairstyle of the female head in no. 11.

Coins could be political propaganda. The victorious racing chariot of no. 11 was meant to advertise the wealth of Syracuse—racing was expensive. Athens' coins (no. 13) stayed the same for a long time. This suggested confidence and stability.

Trade, Seafaring, and Slaves

POOR SOIL AND BARREN MOUNTAINS IN many areas of mainland Greece meant that food and other supplies usually had to be imported. Trade was common, especially by sea. Most ancient Greeks lived near the coast, and often there were mountains and sea separating them from their neighboring towns or villages. Seafaring was therefore frequently the quickest, and sometimes the only, way to travel.

Hazards: shipwreck and piracy

Seafaring was dangerous and also depressing. The earliest known Greek poem, Homer's *Iliad*, tells of the sadness of sailors who are being carried unwillingly out to sea by the winds, away from the inviting gleam of firelight they had left on the shore.

Navigation at night was often done by observing the stars. But this was a system with serious flaws. For example, the stars would tell an experienced sailor his direction but they would not tell him his position or how far he had traveled. So, although he knew that there were dangerous rocks on his route, he would not know how close to them he was. Another problem was that the stars would be covered by cloud just at the time when sailing was especially dangerous, during a storm.

Apart from the danger from a storm or a shipwreck, there was also the real risk of meeting pirates. People were kidnapped by pirates and held for ransom. Some pirates would capture merchant sailors and sell them as slaves in a remote land, never to see their homes and families again. Others would steal the cargo and throw the sailors into the sea. In this way pirates would prevent revenge: dead men could tell no tales.

▲ This slave boy, brought from Africa, is shown cleaning a shoe. Most housework in wealthy homes was done by slaves, who were called "boys" and "girls" even when they were adults.

Sea trade with foreign lands

What did Greek ships carry? Even in Mycenaean times, sailors were going to the ends of the known world to bring back metals. Ships went to Cyprus, Syria, and probably northern Europe to get copper and tin. Together these metals made bronze for the weapons and armor worn by Mycenaean noblemen. As well as keeping them alive in battle, these objects would also intimidate their subjects in peacetime.

One wrecked ship from the Bronze Age has been discovered in the eastern Mediterranean. It was loaded with copper and was probably heading for some Mycenaean Greek town when it was wrecked. In Mycenaean times, as in the classical period, there was trade between Greece and Egypt to supply the Egyptian reed papyrus for writing material.

Food was imported and exported in massive quantities. When in 480 B.C.E. King Xerxes reached the Hellespont, on his march of invasion into Greece, he watched cargo ships bringing grain through the channel for the towns of Greece. The city of Athens, by far the largest in Greece during the classical period, depended so heavily on this grain from the Black Sea coasts that it built a large military navy to protect the cargo ships. Athens paid for the grain with silver from its mines.

The Athenians exported olive oil, wine, and their beautiful painted pottery, much of which traveled as far as northern Italy. The port of Athens—Peiraieus—became the most important market of the Aegean. Many of the goods brought to Peiraieus would be exported again to other towns. Foreign traders who used the port and market paid tax to the Athenians.

An Athenian poet, Hermippos, listed some of the goods that came on cargo ships to Peiraieus. There

◀ Slaves mining with a primitive pick and bucket. A pot of water is lowered, so that they can drink without leaving their work.

▶ A fragment of a late fifth-century B.C.E. inscription on stone from Athens. It records a slave sale. Children were cheap, but strong men and pretty women were expensive.

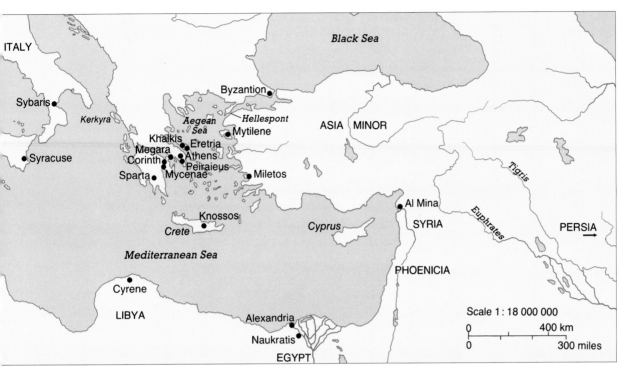

◀ The main ports of Greek trade. Many products came from the Persian Empire, even though relations between Persia and Greece were often hostile. Grain carriers sailed from Athens right to the north of the Black Sea.

▼ An anchor from the wreck of a second-century B.C.E. Greek merchant ship found off north Wales. The sailors came from Alexandria, Egypt, seeking copper, tin, or perhaps gold.

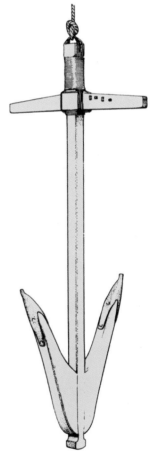

was leather from Cyrene in North Africa, mackerel and other salted fish from the Hellespont, salt and beef from Italy, sails and rope from Egypt, incense from Syria, ivory from Libya, dates and nuts from central Asia Minor, and rugs and pretty cushions from Carthage. Greece was short of suitable timber for the building of Athens' great fleet (see pages 28–29), and this was imported from lands that lay to the north of the Aegean.

The Greek slave trade

Sadly, another frequent cargo was slaves. They were sometimes Greeks who had been captured in war. More often, however, they were non-Greeks, peoples from the fringes of the Greek world. How were they treated, once they had arrived in Greece?

Some slaves won the trust and affection of their owners, while others' lives were unpleasant. Among the most wretched were men made to sweat in the silver mines of Athens, subject to accidents and sometimes kept in leg irons. Many female slaves, and some males, were forced to provide entertainment for citizens who were often drunk or brutal.

More fortunate were the slaves who acted as elementary teachers for the children of wealthy citizens or as police in the assembly of Athens. A few slaves were rewarded with freedom. But for the majority, life meant drudgery such as digging, fetching water, or cleaning.

A slave might escape a beating in public, because passers-by would not like to see it. But out of sight, indoors, or on a farm or in a mine, slaves were often treated with cruelty.

In Athens and in the surrounding land of Attica, it is estimated that there were as many slaves—possibly around 100,000—as there were nonslaves. Poorer people were not able to afford a slave, but it is likely that most farmers made use of some slaves. Slavery was considered acceptable and played a vital role in the economy of most states.

◀ This comedy scene was funnier to the Athenians than it is to us. A slave is dragged by a rope around his neck and threatened with a big stick.

The Spartan Empire

WHEN ATHENS SURRENDERED TO SPARTA in 404 B.C.E., the rich in many Greek states were delighted. Now they could rule. They began by abolishing the democracies that Athens had protected. Countless democrats were put to death. In Athens itself, Spartans demolished the long walls that for 50 years had protected the city from fear of siege, joining it to the sea. Flute girls, entertainers of the rich, played happy music as the walls came crashing down.

The march of the 10,000

When war between Athens and Sparta ended, many Greek soldiers found themselves unemployed. To earn a living, about 10,000 of them went to Mesopotamia (modern Iraq) to fight for a Persian prince, Kyros. But Kyros was killed and the Greek soldiers found themselves abandoned, very far from home in the hostile Persian Empire.

The "10,000" marched northwest, through enemy attacks and foul weather, for about 600 miles (965 km). Only a few of them were killed. At last the men at the front of the marching column shouted in excitement "the sea, the sea!" They had seen the eastern Black Sea, but were still very far from mainland Greece. Being seafarers, however, the Greeks were now confident of getting home. It had taken four months of marching since the death of Kyros, but the nightmare of endless Asia was over.

Sparta's defeat at Leuktra

The survival of the 10,000 suggested that the Persian Empire was weak. Sparta attacked the Persians in Asia Minor, but with little success. Sparta had taken over most of the old Athenian Empire. But Sparta's way of ruling made far more enemies than friends. The Spartans had learned to rule harshly over their Greek helots at home. Perhaps they found it hard to treat other Greeks with the necessary tact and respect. Sparta made sudden attacks, even in peacetime, on Thebes and on Peiraieus, Athens' port. Even Sparta's friends disapproved. Few Greeks were sad when Thebes crushed Sparta's army at the battle of Leuktra. Sparta's empire was over.

Three decades of Spartan rule, 404–371 B.C.E.

404 Athens surrenders, and Sparta takes over the Athenian Empire. Democracy in many cities is replaced by oligarchy —the rule by a wealthy few.

403 Democracy restored at Athens. Athens begins to regain some independence from Sparta.

401–400 The 10,000 march from the heart of the Persian Empire to the Black Sea.

396–394 Sparta campaigns against Persia in Asia Minor.

395–387 Athens and Sparta at war again.

387 Sparta abandons the Greek claim on Asia Minor and allows Persia to dictate peace terms for Greece.

382 Spartan troops seize Thebes.

378 Spartan forces try to seize Peiraieus.

371 Thebes's overwhelming numbers crush Sparta at Leuktra.

▲ Xenophon, who accompanied the 10,000, described the march far into the Persian Empire and back again. He tells how the Greeks despaired and were homesick in Babylonia, but fought their way home through mountains, deep snow, and enemy attacks.

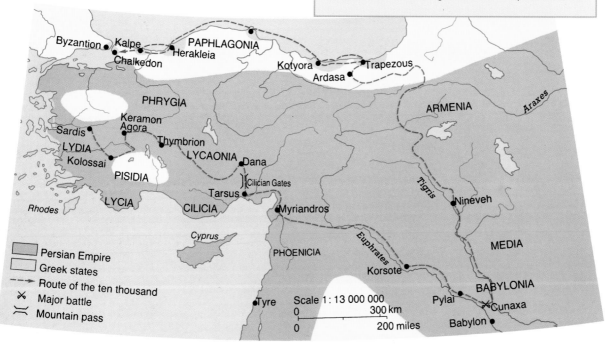

Persian Empire
Greek states
- - - → Route of the ten thousand
✕ Major battle
≍ Mountain pass

Scale 1 : 13 000 000
0   300 km
0   200 miles

◀ The march of the 10,000, 401 B.C.E. To fight his brother Artaxerxes, Prince Kyros employed a Greek army — the best soldiers—and Asian troops. They were led into Babylonia and won the battle of Cunaxa, although Kyros was killed. In spite of a truce, the Persians treacherously killed the Greek leaders, leaving the 10,000 to make their way home via the Greek cities of the Black Sea.

► Many Spartans grew rich from the wealth of the former Athenian Empire, and spent huge sums on breeding and training racehorses, like those shown on this Greek vase. To win a chariot race was a sign of the owner's manliness, even though he hired a charioteer or jockey.

▼ This aerial picture shows the remains of the walls of Messene. They are the best surviving example of fourth-century fortifications. The fortified city was built by Thebes to keep out the Spartans, who never managed to capture it.

Philip and the Rise of Macedon

ONE BY ONE THE GREAT POWERS OF Greece were becoming exhausted. Athens had been weakened by the Peloponnesian Wars and the loss of her empire in 404 B.C.E. In the 350s B.C.E. Athens nearly went bankrupt, trying in vain to hold onto another little empire. Sparta was ruined by the loss of Messenia. After 370 B.C.E. most of Sparta's energy went into futile attempts to get Messenia back.

Phokis, usually an insignificant state and now the enemy of Thebes, seized the enormous treasure of gold at the shrine of Delphi and melted it down to make coins. This money bought an army of mercenary soldiers for Phokis, and the army wore down Thebes in a long war.

Away to the northeast of the Greek mainland was the partly Greek kingdom of Macedon (Macedonia). Its ruler was King Philip—an extremely ambitious man who was probably watching the decline of Thebes with satisfaction.

▶ The restless Philip ("horse-lover") of Macedon, shown on one of his own coins. Philip moved swiftly from one conquest to the next; the horse may perhaps suggest this speed.

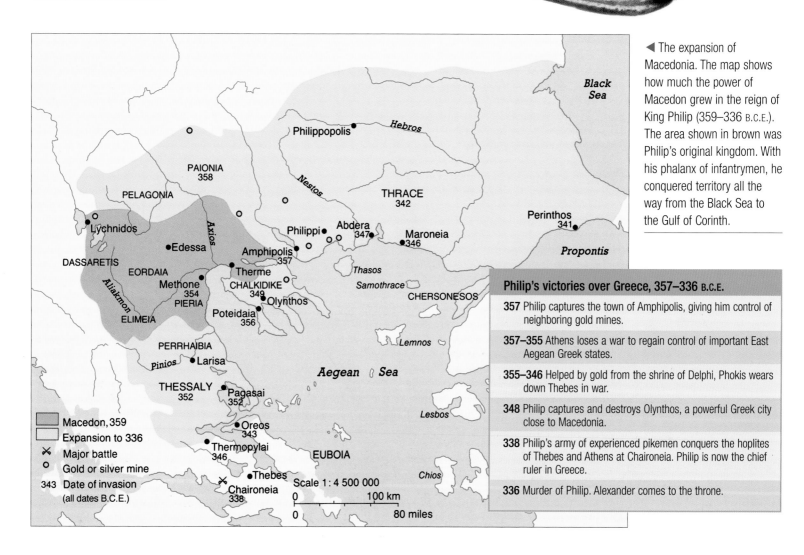

◀ The expansion of Macedonia. The map shows how much the power of Macedon grew in the reign of King Philip (359–336 B.C.E.). The area shown in brown was Philip's original kingdom. With his phalanx of infantrymen, he conquered territory all the way from the Black Sea to the Gulf of Corinth.

Map legend

- ▨ Macedon, 359
- ☐ Expansion to 336
- ✕ Major battle
- ○ Gold or silver mine
- 343 Date of invasion (all dates B.C.E.)

Scale 1 : 4 500 000

0 — 100 km
0 — 80 miles

Philip's victories over Greece, 357–336 B.C.E.

357 Philip captures the town of Amphipolis, giving him control of neighboring gold mines.

357–355 Athens loses a war to regain control of important East Aegean Greek states.

355–346 Helped by gold from the shrine of Delphi, Phokis wears down Thebes in war.

348 Philip captures and destroys Olynthos, a powerful Greek city close to Macedonia.

338 Philip's army of experienced pikemen conquers the hoplites of Thebes and Athens at Chaironeia. Philip is now the chief ruler in Greece.

336 Murder of Philip. Alexander comes to the throne.

◀ A copy of a sculpture of King Philip of Macedonia from the fourth century B.C.E. Philip was the father of Alexander the Great, who succeeded him to the throne (see pages 46–47).

Philip conquers the Greek mainland

Philip, like the Phokians, gained great power because of his large supply of gold. From the 350s B.C.E. onward the gold mines of Philippi enabled him to raise a mercenary army. His soldiers acquired valuable experience and conquered much territory because they campaigned all the year round. In contrast, most Greek states could only afford to send out hoplites for emergency campaigns, and their soldiers were only part-time.

▼ Philip's main force in battle was made up of heavily armed footsoldiers. They fought much like Greek hoplites (see pages 30–31), but used a longer, heavier spear called a *sarissa*.

Philip's men fought their way east toward the Black Sea and south into Thessaly. Their progress was made easier by another, secret, use of Philip's gold. He was using it to bribe politicians in Greek cities to support him.

In about 339 or 338 B.C.E. Philip was finally ready to confront the main Greek powers. He led his army across Thessaly, through the pass of Thermopylai, and proceeded into Boiotia. There, at a place called Chaironeia, he fought the combined armies of Thebes and Athens—and won. His most influential enemy, Demosthenes of Athens, took part in the battle but ran away defeated. Philip was now overlord of the Greek mainland.

Philip treated Athens and Thebes fairly gently. (But after Philip's death his son, Alexander the Great, destroyed Thebes for having dared to revolt.) Philip was probably hoping for Greek support, and especially the help of Athens' navy, in a war that he was planning against the Persian Empire. But in 336 B.C.E., back in Macedonia, Philip was murdered. His son Alexander was now in charge. A young man, his task was to tackle Persia.

Philip's victory is often seen as the end of Greek independence. Greece was now ruled by Macedonian generals, or rather by the fear of them. Greek cities still sometimes fought each other. But to the Macedonians, fighting elsewhere for far greater stakes, the battles of the Greeks seemed as unimportant as the scuffling of mice.

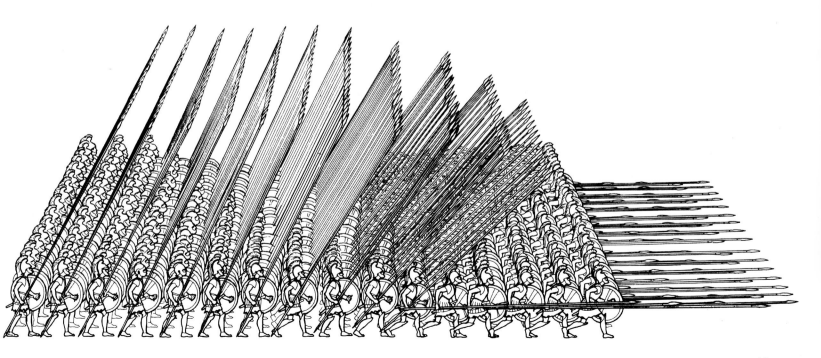

Royal Tombs of Macedon

AT VERGINA IN MACEDONIA ARCHAEOLOGISTS excavating in 1977 discovered underground tombs, expensively built of marble and containing treasure. In one tomb they found parts of the skeleton and skull of someone who had been cremated. Obviously, they are most likely to be the remains of a rich and very powerful individual. But of whom? None of the graves that were uncovered contains any inscription to tell us.

Who was the soldier in the tomb?

The body is certainly not that of Alexander. He died in the east, and for centuries his body could be seen (embalmed—he was not cremated) at Alexandria in Egypt. Scientists have examined the skull from Vergina and seem to have found a clue as to whose it was. The skull shows signs of a serious wound above the right eye. And this is what an ancient Greek writer said of King Philip, Alexander's father:

"His right eye was cut out when he was hit by an arrow while inspecting the siege-engines and the protection sheds at the siege of Methone."

This siege took place in 354 B.C.E., and Philip was lucky to survive. An ivory model head found in a royal grave at Vergina also has an unusual groove over the right eye. It is probably a portrait of Philip, and the body in the grave may be his.

▲ Vergina, site of the royal burials, is some distance from Pella, capital of Macedonia. Also shown is Methone, which Philip captured. He was injured in the process.

▶ Grave goods at Vergina. To the right of the bronze shield cover are leg guards, and to their right is a gold diadem, or crown, a symbol of royal authority.

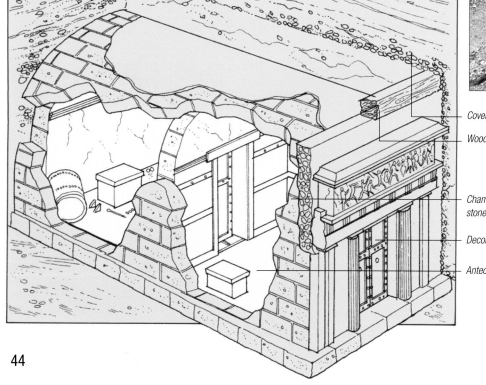

Covering of earth

Wooden beams

Chamber of carefully carved stones

Decorative entrance

Antechamber

◀ The entrance to the main tombs at Vergina, reconstructed. Running above the marble columns, traces of a frieze showing a lion-hunt can still be seen. Below it are bright bands of blue paint. This "palace of the underworld" is like earlier Mycenaean tombs.

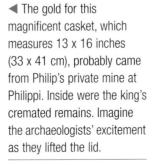

▲ Gleaming after more than 2,300 years, the gold quiver shows (at top right) an archer. The bronze leg guards are of different lengths.

▲ An ivory head from Vergina, which may show Alexander, Philip's son.

◄ The gold for this magnificent casket, which measures 13 x 16 inches (33 x 41 cm), probably came from Philip's private mine at Philippi. Inside were the king's cremated remains. Imagine the archaeologists' excitement as they lifted the lid.

Appropriately for Philip, the goods found buried at Vergina reflect a soldierly life. Our illustrations show a great shield cover, and leg guards made of bronze. A pair of greaves (guards for the lower leg) is of uneven length. One is about 1 inch (2.5 cm) shorter than the other. It is known from ancient written evidence that Philip was slightly lame. These greaves may, then, have been specially made for him. They were buried with him in case he should need them in his life after death in the underworld.

It is not absolutely certain that the skull and bones in the tomb are those of Philip. The medical evidence has been contested, and it has been suggested that the remains may be those of a half-brother of Alexander.

What is certain, however, is the rarity of finding an ancient burial place intact—one that has not been looted. That Vergina escaped being looted is due in part to the large mound of earth with which the grave was covered.

Philip's murder—who ordered it?

Philip had been murdered at his court in Macedonia, where people had gathered for the celebration of the marriage of his daughter. He was stabbed by one of his bodyguards. The killer was himself quickly killed, and his motives are very uncertain.

It is sometimes suspected that Olympias, the first wife of Philip and mother of Alexander, helped plot the murder. She had good reason to resent the king. He had had a son by a later wife, and this younger son might have threatened to exclude Alexander from succeeding to the throne.

Alexander's Campaigns

AT PHILIP'S DEATH, ALEXANDER BECAME king of Macedonia. But the outlook for the new king was not good. He was very young, only 20, and physically small. "Just a boy," his enemies said. He was also short of money—his father had left large debts. But Alexander did not give up Philip's hugely ambitious plan. He would try to conquer the Persian Empire.

Alexander probably reasoned like this. Persian troops had regularly been defeated by Greek hoplites. In 401–400 B.C.E. the Greek army of 10,000 had marched across the Persian Empire (see page 40). But until the time of Philip and Alexander, no phalanx had been large enough to conquer Persia permanently. Now that Macedonia controlled most of Greece, a devastating phalanx could be put together.

Alexander in Egypt and Persia

Leading about 24,000 heavily armed infantry—half from Greece, half from Macedonia—Alexander crossed the Hellespont into Asia Minor in 334 B.C.E. Winning his first battle against the Persians, at the Granikos River, he headed for Phoenicia, the heart of Persia's naval power. Victorious there and in Egypt, he then moved eastward to the center of Persia's land power.

At Gaugamela, beyond the Tigris River, Alexander fought for control of the Persian Empire. His opponent, King Darius, had a far larger army. But Alexander's troops had the discipline to withstand even the Persian war chariots. After savage fighting, Darius fled and was killed by some of his own men. Alexander was emperor. He was not content, however. He wanted to conquer India.

Alexander advances into India

Victory in India would bring him, Alexander thought, to the end of the world. His men defeated one Indian army and its deadly weapon—war elephants. But the prospect of crossing Indian desert and fighting more elephants was too much. The army would go no farther. For Alexander to have led his men as he did was a superb achievement. They must often have despaired of ever seeing home again.

The reign of Alexander, 336–323 B.C.E.

336 Alexander inherits the kingdom of Macedonia and overlordship of Greece.

335 Thebes revolts but Alexander destroys it.

334 Alexander invades and conquers Asia Minor.

333 Victory at Issos—Alexander enters Phoenicia.

332 Conquest of Syria and Egypt.

331 Foundation of Alexandria in Egypt. Defeat of King Darius by Alexander at Gaugamela.

330–327 Alexander founds many cities in the eastern parts of the former Persian Empire.

326 Alexander enters India and conquers Punjab. His army refuses to go farther.

323 Alexander dies at Babylon. His empire is divided.

▼ The conquests of Alexander. An enormous area of land was won by Alexander's army. By comparison, the Greek mainland is tiny. The soldiers marched so far partly out of respect for Alexander— they knew that he fought his enemies with the utmost courage.

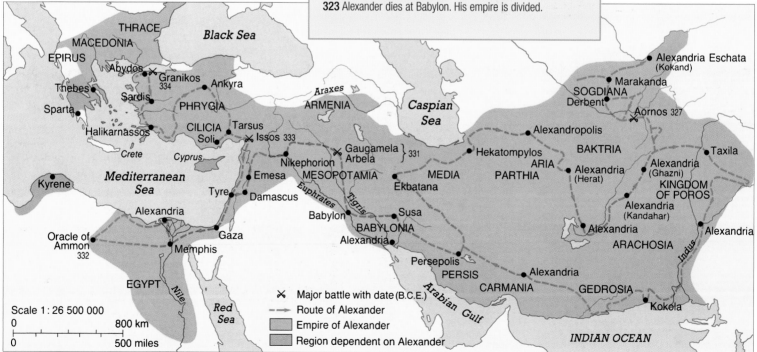

× Major battle with date (B.C.E.)
--- - → Route of Alexander
Empire of Alexander
Region dependent on Alexander

Scale 1: 26 500 000

▶ Alexander's men fight the elephants of King Poros in northwest India. The animals were trained to trample their opponents and shield their own side.

▼ Alexander wanted his power to seem godlike. Here he is shown wearing a ramshorn cap—symbol of the ancient Egyptian god Ammon.

▼ A miniature sculpture of a war elephant, with an enemy soldier between its tusks. Alexander's army met war elephants in India, and feared them greatly. Alexander's successors swapped a huge part of their eastern territory for a herd of these trained beasts to fight for them.

◀ To keep the peace in his empire, Alexander wanted his Greek and non-Greek peoples to integrate. He himself married an easterner, and he made many of his men do the same.

This silver disk, from remote Afghanistan, shows how Greek and non-Greek ideas were blended. On the left in Greek dress is the goddess Kybele. A figure in eastern dress shelters her with a parasol. Also eastern are the sun god in the sky and the priest (right) at a fire altar.

The Successor Kingdoms

WHEN ALEXANDER DIED OF ILLNESS HE was only 32. But he had long foreseen that his empire would face serious problems. Greek-speakers had commonly despised the people ruled by Persia, calling them barbarians and slavish worshipers of an emperor. But now they had to rule these people. If they acted arrogantly, they might cause their subjects to revolt.

To prevent this from happening, Alexander married an eastern aristocrat named Roxane. He made many of his men do likewise. He hoped to breed a future aristocracy that would be both Greek and eastern by descent, and would respect both sides. He had little success. At his death, many of his men divorced their eastern wives.

The end of Alexander's empire

Like many kings, Alexander also faced the problem of who would rule after his death. The fear was of civil war, as rivals fought for the throne. The traditional solution was to produce a son and heir. But Alexander's son by Roxane was too young at the time of his father's death. Alexander's former generals saw the child as a threat. Both the boy and his mother were murdered, and the generals split up the empire among themselves.

The largest territory went to Seleukos. He was to rule from Syria and Palestine in the west to the frontier lands of India in the east. It was Seleukos who gave up territory within India in exchange for 500 war elephants.

Although the empire of the Seleukids shrank over the course of the next two centuries, the deadly elephant herd remained—until Rome ordered the animals to be crippled in 163 B.C.E. Smaller kingdoms with Greek-speaking rulers were carved from Alexander's former lands, such as Baktria in the east and Pergamon in Asia Minor.

The longest-lasting kingdom was set up by Alexander's former general Ptolemy. He, followed by his family, ruled Egypt. The crops along the Nile River made Egypt extremely rich, and the deserts to east and west made it relatively easy to defend. The capital, Alexandria, became the most important city in the Greek-speaking world. The last Ptolemy to rule Egypt was the famous Queen Cleopatra, who lost her kingdom to Rome in 31 B.C.E.

The Greeks' lasting influence

Alexander's conquests spread the Greek language and lifestyle among the wealthy and educated classes of the former Persian Empire. For example, Jesus and his first followers (poor men) spoke Aramaic, a non-Greek language. But when the New Testament was written, for more prosperous people who could read, it was in Greek. (The Greek word for Greece was *Hellas*. The new civilization is called Hellenistic because it was Hellenized—made Greek.)

Perhaps the best work done by Hellenistic thinkers was in science and technology. Gears, cog wheels, steam engines, and slot machines were made. Eratosthenes was roughly right in his calculation

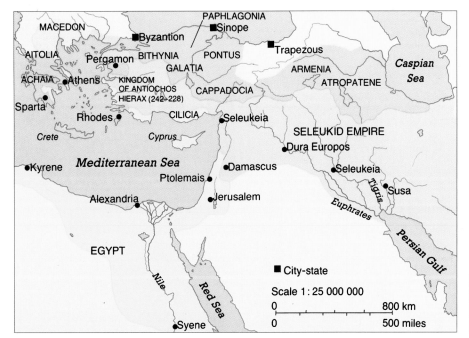

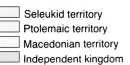

◀ The Hellenistic world in 240 B.C.E. The rulers of Macedonia have long ago lost control of the Asiatic lands conquered by Alexander, and also of much of Greece. Asia Minor has fragmented. But the Seleukids and Ptolemies still keep great empires.

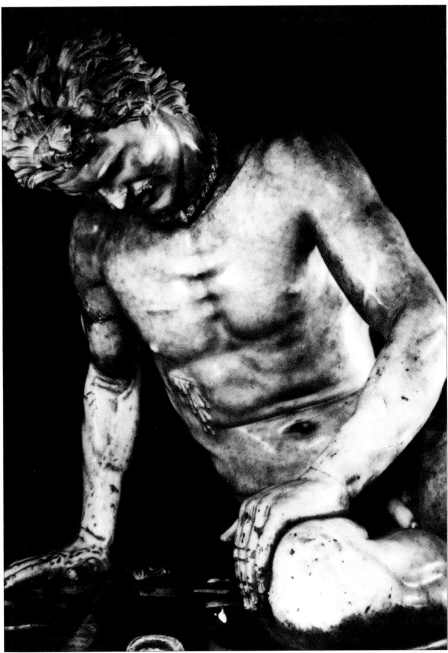

▲ A Pergamene statue of a dying Celt, with blood oozing from his wounds. Pergamon, a Hellenistic kingdom, was proud to defeat a Celtic army.

◀ This Hellenistic rock-cut tomb, 130 ft (40 m) high, is at Petra. The columns, in Greek style, are in a non-Greek setting—a cliff face.

of the circumference of the earth. Aristarchos, unlike other scientists, understood that earth went around the Sun. What did not survive in the Hellenistic age was the society based upon the Greek city-state, with citizens serving as soldiers and, as in Athens, enjoying public debates and voting to make important decisions.

Although most of the Hellenistic lands were conquered by Rome, Greek-speakers kept their influence, by teaching the Romans. In 330 C.E. the capital of the Roman Empire was moved to a Greek city—Constantinople (formerly Byzantion).

Part Two

Culture and Society

▲ A bronze mask—a version of the mask a tragic actor would wear for a performance in the fifth century B.C.E.

▶ The Akropolis ("High City") at Athens.

Inset Key to the maps on pages 52–59.

N.W. Greece

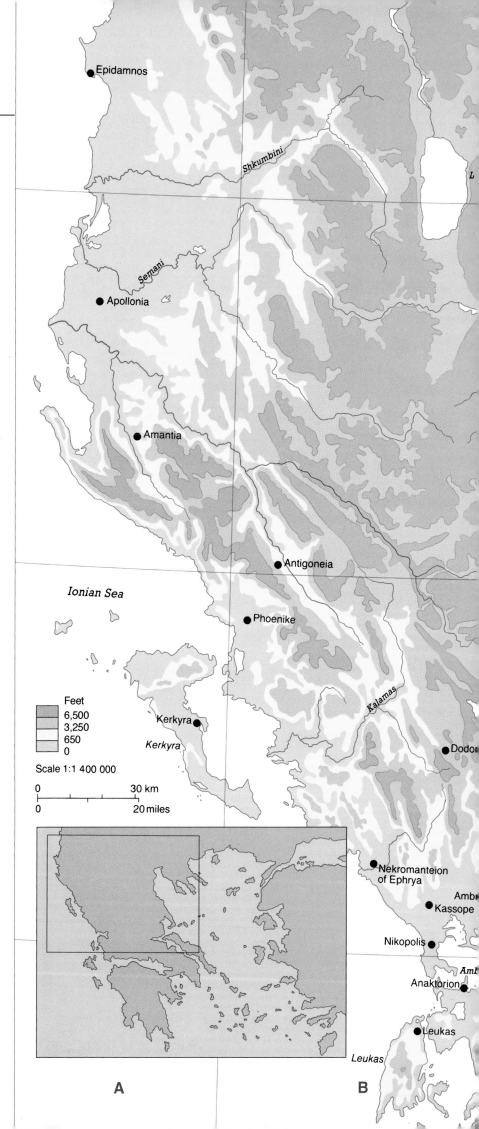

S OME OF THE MOST MOUNTAINOUS PARTS of Greece lie in the northwestern region. From north to south runs the great Pindos range of mountains. Farther east is the towering Mount Olympos. In such areas little would grow, and the population was too small and too poor to contribute much to the development of Greek civilization.

For Greeks far away in the main cities these remote and mysterious mountain areas seemed a likely place for gods to inhabit. Mount Olympos was seen as the home of the gods, and to the oracle at Dodone came many Greeks from distant communities, to question Zeus and the goddess Dione about the future.

The island of Kerkyra (Corfu)

Kerkyra could be reached more rapidly from the main Greek cities—by sea. Colonized by Corinth in the eighth century B.C.E., Kerkyra by the 430s B.C.E. had one of the largest navies in Greece. But vicious civil war between rich and poor on Kerkyra weakened the community, and Kerkyra never played a large part in the interstate affairs of Greece.

The eastern mainland—Thessaly

Thessaly also had less power than its wealth might have allowed. It had the advantage of large areas of flat fertile land, but its politics were somewhat primitive. Even during the classical period it was ruled by a lawless group of rich men. Thessaly's plains were enclosed by mountains and there was only one suitable harbor, based at Pagasai in the fifth and fourth centuries B.C.E. Perhaps the chief role of the flat lands of Thessaly was to be a route for other people's armies, marching to or from the main Greek cities farther south.

The largest of these armies was the force of King Xerxes of Persia in 480 B.C.E. But, after sweeping through Thessaly, Xerxes found himself blocked for a time. This was at Thermopylai (or Pylai). *Pylai* meant "gates." At Thermopylai a narrow strip of land between mountains and sea made a good defense against invaders. It formed the gateway to central Greece. Our maps show the coastline as it is today.

The partly Greek kingdom of Macedonia, on the northeastern mainland, won great power from the 350s B.C.E. Its ruler Philip (father of Alexander the Great) had gold mines in the area; his gold hired soldiers and bribed Greek politicians. When Philip passed through the "gateway" at Thermopylai, in 339 or 338, it was to conquer Greece.

Megali
Prespa

Mikri
Prespa

L Vegorritis

Pella

Axios

Strymon

Amphipolis

Strymonic
Gulf

Thessaloniki

Keletron

Vergina

Stageira

Methone

Aliakmon

Pydna

Olynthos

Dion

Poteidaia

Thermaic
Gulf

△ Mt Olympos

Gonnos

Pinios

MOUNTAINS

Larisa

Kerkineon

Gomphoi

Peirasia

Northern Sporades

Pheria

Iolkos

Metropolis

Pagasai

Koropi

Alos

Istiala

Amphilochian
Argos

Euboia

Gulf of Euboia

Thermopylai

Stratos

Elataia

C

D

E

1

2

3

4

S.W. Greece

IN CRETE AND SOUTHERN GREECE WERE THE great Mediterranean centers of Bronze Age civilization. Crete, with its Minoan culture, had its famous palaces at Knossos and elsewhere. When power shifted away from Crete, it was to palaces of the Peloponnese, such as those at Mycenae and Pylos. These palaces fell around the year 1200 B.C.E., and a dark age followed.

The two chief powers that emerged in the following archaic age and dominated the classical period were Athens and Sparta. Athens grew rich from its silver mines at nearby Laureion, as well as from farming and from trade. It had a magnificent natural harbor at Peiraieus. It sheltered the navy that guarded Athens' merchant ships and won an empire in the Aegean.

Athens' neighbors

West of Athens was Boiotia. Its inhabitants became famous for being dull-witted. But it was Boiotians who at last discovered how to beat the Spartan army. After crushing Sparta in 371 B.C.E. at the battle of Leuktra, Boiotia for a brief period dominated Greece.

Aigina, an island south of Athens, was a famous trading state and naval power in the sixth and early fifth centuries B.C.E. Athens resented and feared Aigina, calling it "the eyesore of the Peiraieus." In 431 B.C.E. Athenians expelled the population of Aigina. Two other neighboring states, Corinth and Megara, survived the enmity of Athens. They were on the mainland, and so could be defended by the land army of Sparta.

Placed on a narrow neck of land, between two seas, Corinth traded with east and west. It founded colonies in western Greece and Sicily, but also in the Aegean. Ancient Corinthians built a trackway of stone to drag ships over the neck of land from the Corinthian Gulf to the Aegean. (The Corinth Canal is a modern, 19th-century development.)

Sparta

Isolated in the southern Peloponnese, Sparta built up its secretive and deadly army. Often competing with Athens, Sparta dominated the southern Peloponnese after 600 B.C.E. and became the most powerful Greek city after the Peloponnesian Wars (see page 32). Spartans drew their wealth from a huge population of Greek serfs, called helots (see pages 22–23). Cut off by sea to the south and by mountains on all other sides, the helots had nowhere to run. Sparta had them at its mercy.

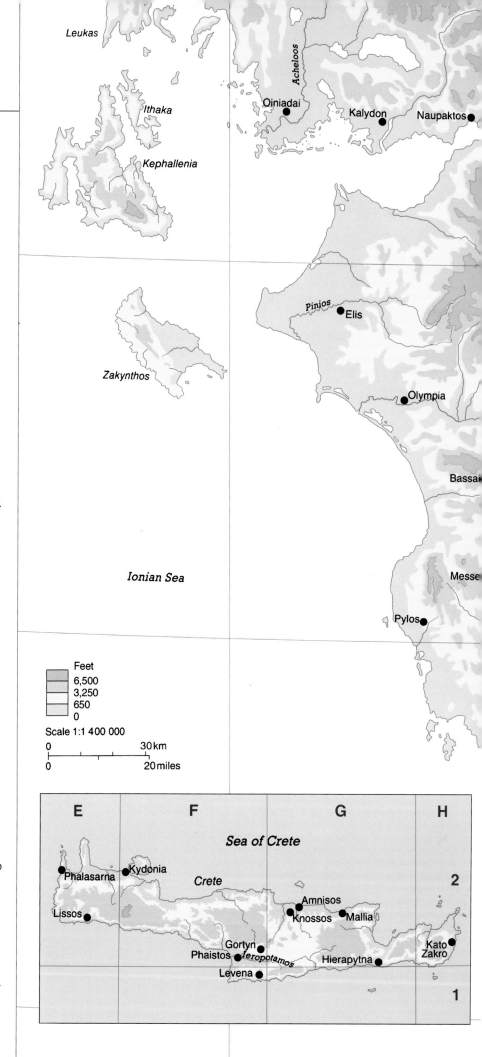

N.E. Greece

E VEN WITHOUT KNOWING MUCH OF THE
history of Greece, you could probably point to
a strategic place on this map where battles
were likely to happen. This is the long narrow
channel, the Hellespont, leading from the Aegean
Sea into the Propontis (Sea of Marmara) and toward
the Black Sea.

Since prehistoric times merchant ships trading
between these seas have threaded their way through
the Hellespont. Also, land armies moving between
Asia and Europe have found the Hellespont a
convenient crossing. Control of this channel was of
immense importance, and was often fought over.

Battles to control the Hellespont

The best-known war in Greek myth happened at
Troy, a town well placed to control the western end
of the Hellespont. There may really have been such a
war, around 1200 B.C.E. (see pages 14–15). Some 600
years later Athens fought against men from the isle
of Lesbos for control of Sigeion, near the site of Troy.
In 480 B.C.E. the Persian army crossed the Hellespont
from south to north on a bridge of boats.

For most of the fifth century B.C.E. the Hellespont
was patrolled by the navy of Athens. It guarded
merchant ships bringing grain from the coasts of the
Black Sea to feed the population of Athens. When
the great war between Athens and Sparta ended in
405 or 404 B.C.E., it was not as a result of a battle on
the Greek mainland but in the Hellespont. Here at
Aigospotamoi, Sparta captured the Athenian fleet
and cut off Athens' supply of food.

In 334 B.C.E. King Alexander of Macedon crossed
the Hellespont with a partly Greek army, this time
from north to south. He was on his way to conquer
the Persian Empire but made a point of first visiting
Troy to pay homage to the Greek military tradition
that he sought to imitate.

Control of northern Greece

In the preceding decades King Philip had extended
his power from Macedonia in the northwest through
Thrace along the northern coast of the Aegean. Most
importantly, at Philippi—to the northwest of the
island of Thasos—he won control of gold mines
that funded his expansion. In the three-pronged
peninsula of Chalkidike in 348 B.C.E., Philip
conquered the powerful city of Olynthos, then
demolished it—all except its foundations. These
now help us understand how Greeks built their
town houses (see pages 90–91).

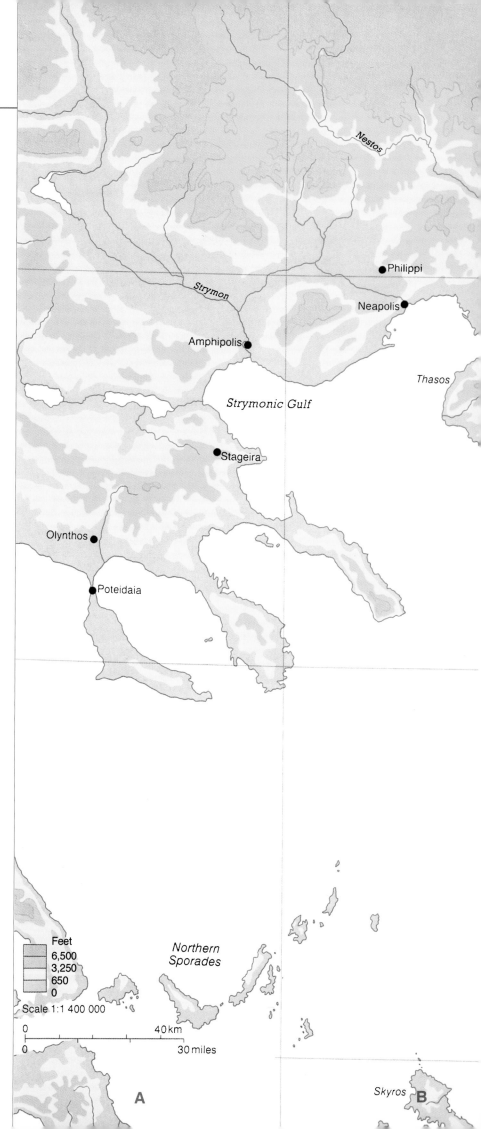

S.E. Greece

A CHAIN OF ISLANDS LIES BETWEEN THE Greek mainland in the west and the coast of Asia Minor in the east. Nowadays tourists use them for "island hopping." In 490 B.C.E., a Persian invasion force used the islands as stepping stones when it moved westward for the attack on Athens at a place called Marathon.

The Ionian Greeks of Asia Minor

Most of the Asia Minor coast shown here was known to the Greeks as Ionia. Ionian Greeks were among the most creative people ever. Their ideas influenced the history of Greece, and of Europe in general. Pythagoras, the mathematician, lived on Samos. Philosophy was invented in Ionia by such men as Anaximandros of Miletos and Xenophanes of Kolophon. Herodotos of Halikarnassos wrote the first large work of history.

Some of the thoughtfulness that characterized these Ionians resulted from their geographical position. In its great days, the sixth and early fifth centuries B.C.E., Ionia was very close to—for a time it was actually part of—the Persian Empire. Like most other Greeks, the Ionians lived on or near the coast. But their neighbors to the east were non-Greek peoples, subjects of Persia. Trade with the Persian east brought Ionians into contact with some of the most sophisticated cultures of the time: those of Egypt and Babylonia.

Awareness of these foreign cultures helped the Ionians ask useful questions. Why was Greek religion so different from foreign religions? How did Greek and Persian political systems differ? Pythagoras may well have got some of his mathematical ideas from the Babylonians. Anaxagoras, the first Greek writer to explain eclipses correctly, was probably using some of the ideas of Babylonian astronomers.

The island communities

Persia lost control of the Ionian coast soon after 479 B.C.E. From then until 405 B.C.E. the navy of Athens dominated most of the area shown on the map. The largest, most powerful island communities within the Athenian Empire were those of Samos, Chios, and Lesbos (see map on page 57).

Islands that rebelled, such as Naxos and Lesbos, paid a heavy penalty when Athens crushed their uprisings. They had to give up much of their land to Athenian settlers. Ionia was handed back to the Persians by Sparta after the defeat of Athens, but Alexander the Great later freed it once more.

A   B

Knossos and Santorini

KNOSSOS IN CRETE WAS ONE OF THE Western world's earliest cities. During its great age, from just after 2000 until about 1400 B.C.E., it had small, two-storied houses packed along narrow streets. About 20 miles (32 km) away was its port, Amnisos, through which went the precious trade with Egypt and Syria. The population of Knossos and Amnisos may have reached 100,000, an extremely large number for that time.

Knossos has been a major archaeological site since its palace was first excavated by a British archaeologist, Arthur Evans, in 1900. Digging at the site has revealed evidence of a sophisticated culture, one that benefited from a system of running water carried in clay pipes.

The palace at Knossos

Knossos contained a palace that was built not on a single grand design but with very many small rooms added as the need arose. Twice the palace was wrecked by earthquakes, but it was not heavily fortified against enemies, unlike the later Mycenaean palaces built on the Greek mainland. Although the rulers of Knossos may not have spoken Greek, their

▲ The modern town of Thera (Santorini), built on the rim of the former volcano. The remarkable Bronze Age site was on the other side of the island, at Akrotiri.

◄ Section of the palace of Knossos, partly restored. Later Greek myth told of the powerful King Minos of Crete and a monstrous minotaur, half-man, half-bull. Now archaeology has proved that bulls were prominent in Cretan life and art. Notice the model bulls' horns in stone (left).

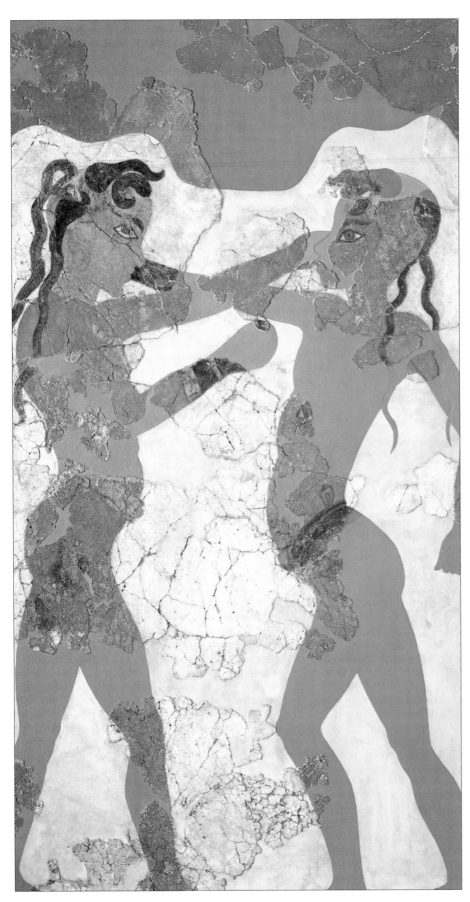

◄ Two boys boxing, in a painting from Santorini. Their tanned skin is shown in red.

▲ One of several paintings from Santorini showing an interest in animals. This one shows antelope.

dress and art were copied by the Mycenaean Greeks. Wall paintings show Cretan ladies wearing low-cut dresses with puffed sleeves and flounced skirts. So many women are shown in these paintings that it seems likely that women were unusually influential in this peaceful society.

Remains of houses on Santorini

Santorini (Thera in Greek) is a volcanic island of the southern Aegean. Excavations there since 1967 have uncovered remains of wealthy houses from about 1500 B.C.E., with magnificent wall paintings in the style of Minoan Crete and of Mycenae. They were overwhelmed by lava in a large volcanic eruption, probably when they were relatively new.

Many of the wall paintings form a remarkable set telling a pictorial story. Long, low warships with brightly colored canopies set off on a raid. Dolphins leap in the surrounding sea. Arriving at a coastal town, the raiders conquer its defenders, some of whom are shown drowning.

In the enemy town are women and animals. Capturing them was very likely the purpose of the raid. Back at their own town, the raiders are welcomed by a crowd of men. Women watch from a flat roof. Some of the raiders wear boars' tusk helmets in the Mycenaean style. This story of a naval raid, with important female characters, is similar to later Homeric tales of Mycenaean warriors. They too cross the sea to make war—to capture Helen of Troy.

Palaces at Mycenae and Pylos

THE ARCHAEOLOGY OF GREECE SEEMS TO tell us most about the wealthiest people. This is because their buried possessions lasted, whereas the possessions of the poor did not. For example, the rich had great stone houses, whereas the poor had little houses of mud. Rich women wore gold; poor women wore flowers. Archaeologists can find stone ruins and gold objects but the mud houses and the flowers are gone.

At Mycenae and Pylos Greek rulers, living in rambling palaces of stone, enjoyed far more treasure than had ever been known in Greece before. So many fine things survived from their palaces—even to today, more than 3,000 years later—that we can begin to imagine the splendor in which the rulers must have lived. In contrast, the poor of the Mycenaean world seem hard to trace, until we remember that it was humble people—builders, artists, metalworkers, and stonecarvers—who created the palaces and treasures.

The riches of Mycenae

Mycenae stood on a low hill in the northeastern Peloponnese. From their palace on the hilltop, the rulers of the town could keep an eye on their subjects below. Stretching away from Mycenae to the south was the road to a fine natural harbor, through which came the materials of wealth: copper and tin to make bronze weapons, gold and amber for jewelry, ivory for carving, and papyrus for making written records. Being only a few miles from the sea, Mycenae was well placed to trade and to send out warships. But, set a little back from the coast, the town had some protection against sudden raids by seaborne pirates.

From about 1600 B.C.E. craftsmen were using gold to make death masks for rulers of Mycenae. Royal corpses could now lie with handsome faces that would gleam for ever.

Other artists specialized in showing curves, in a style adapted from that of Minoan Crete. Look at the "waists" of the lions above the famous gateway of Mycenae (below), and (right) at the curves on the female figures carved in ivory. The stone roofs of the gigantic beehive tombs, in which later Mycenaean rulers were laid to rest, were curved too.

Pylos: wealthy harbor town

Pylos, in the southwestern Peloponnese, was also near a natural harbor—one of the best in Greece. Like Mycenae, the palace of Pylos had its store of inscriptions written on clay, to record how supplies had been distributed.

Clay tablets also refer to the maintenance of guards on the coast, probably as defense against an attack by sea. Such an attack may have destroyed the palace. Luxuries found at Pylos include a bath, in which the ruler may have sat while female slaves washed him. There is also decorative ivory, skillfully set into wood.

◀ The Lion Gate, the main entrance in the massive defensive wall of Mycenae. The picture shows the gate as 19th-century archaeologists found it. Clearing away the earth and fallen stones has shown the gate to be much taller than it appears here.

▲ The famous golden death mask from the royal graves at Mycenae. When the German archaeologist Schliemann found it, he thought in his excitement that it showed the face of the legendary King Agamemnon. This now seems unlikely, however.

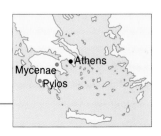

▲ Two women and a child, carved in ivory at Mycenae in the 13th century B.C.E. Notice the women's necklaces and—below the waist—their extravagant flounced clothing in the Minoan style.

▼ This simple but elegant vessel is of bronze—Mycenaean culture belongs to the late Bronze Age. Bronze (an alloy of tin and copper) was then the strongest metal known for weapons and tools.

▶ A wall painting from Pylos showing soldiers killing barbarian enemies. The Pylian soldiers wear helmets made from boars' tusks. Their enemies wear animal skins.

Myths of Blood

GREEK MYTHS ARE FAMOUS FOR THEIR violence and sexual adventure. Some of the best known are tales of murderous revenge by ruling families such as that of Atreus of Mycenae. Sometimes the murdered are avenged by spirits.

Atreus and Thyestes
The wife of Atreus had an affair with Thyestes, Atreus's brother. So Atreus killed Thyestes' three sons and served him their flesh as part of a meal. Thyestes ate it. Atreus gloatingly told him what he had eaten. Thyestes fled, but later had another son, Aigisthos, who killed Atreus.

Agamemnon and Klytaimnestra
The two sons of Atreus were Agamemnon and Menelaos, who led the war against Troy (see pages 14–15). To gain a favorable wind to take ships to Troy, Agamemnon killed his own daughter as a sacrifice to Artemis. Bitterly angry, Klytaimnestra—Agamemnon's wife and mother of the dead girl—took as her lover Aigisthos, the killer of Agamemnon's father.

Knowing nothing of this affair, Agamemnon returned glorious from Troy with a lover of his own. Klytaimnestra met the couple, invited them inside the royal palace with gracious words, and then hacked them to death.

This created another problem, because Orestes, the son of Agamemnon and Klytaimnestra, needed to avenge his father by killing his mother. This he did, but he was pursued by the dark spirits who avenged murdered people—the Furies.

▲ A coin with the head of the hero Herakles looking out from the jaws of a lion—the man-eating Nemean lion that Herakles had to kill.

▶ Elektra lifts the ax to kill Klytaimnestra, her mother. Elektra, with her brother Orestes, killed her to avenge their father's murder which Klytaimnestra had planned.

▼ Agamemnon's murder, shown on an Athenian vase. In this version the killing is done by Aigisthos, urged on by Klytaimnestra, wife of Agamemnon. On the right is Agamemnon's new lover.

The magical tale of Odysseus
Odysseus was an ally of Agamemnon. The *Odyssey* tells of his reluctant voyaging after the fall of Troy, when storms drove him to remote and magical lands. Some of his men were eaten by a one-eyed monster, the Cyclops. Others were sucked to their deaths by the whirlpool Charybdis.

Odysseus was forced to spend nights with the beautiful nymph Kalypso. But by day he sat weeping for his wife, Penelope. She waited patiently at home until he eventually returned. Fortunately, Odysseus had the goddess Athena on his side and she asked Zeus to ensure that Kalypso released Odysseus.

▶ Helped by the goddess Athena (left), Perseus slays the Gorgon. One hand grips the monster by her snake-wreathed head, while the other hand cuts her throat.

▼ Pentheus, mortal ruler of Thebes, made war against the god Dionysos. In revenge the god's female followers, the Mainads ("ravers"), tore him to pieces.

After 10 years Odysseus came home and, killing the men who claimed her, won Penelope back.

The heroes Herakles and Perseus

These two men were famed for freeing mankind from monsters. The lion of Nemea ate people and cattle until Herakles strangled it with his bare hands. He made its skin into a cloak, its head serving as his helmet. He also killed the Hydra, a snake with many heads that grew again when they were cut off. The Hydra's breath poisoned the countryside until Herakles cut off its heads and sealed the many necks with fire before more heads could grow.

Perseus had the task of killing the Gorgon, a female monster who turned people to stone as their eyes met. Perseus used a polished shield to act as a mirror and cut off the Gorgon's head without looking directly at her. Perseus also saved the beautiful Andromeda who was chained to a rock. Her own parents planned to sacrifice her to a sea monster in order to save their kingdom from the anger of the god of the sea, Poseidon. Perseus killed the monster and then married Andromeda.

Gods and Goddesses of Olympos

TALES OF THE GODS AND GODDESSES OF Greece are now told for fun. Gods who fall in love with mortal women, or goddesses who fight in men's battles, make good entertainment.

Greeks found them entertaining, too. Storytellers were free to make up many details of what the various divinities did. But they had to show respect. If offended, gods and goddesses could inflict terrible punishment on the perpetrator. Most Greeks, it seems, were afraid of the gods.

Explaining the physical world

The idea of the supernatural was used to explain processes that were not fully understood. Why did dark clouds bring rain, thunder, and lightning? It

▶ Hermes, messenger of the gods, puts on his winged sandals. He will then take off from Olympos and fly—as Greeks obviously dreamed of being able to do.

▼ Mount Olympos in northeast Greece is more than 9,500 ft (2,800 m) high. The *Iliad* and *Odyssey* describe it as the home of the gods. They lived in luxury in a palace with a bronze floor.

must be a sky god at work—Zeus. Why would crops not grow in winter? It must be because the earth goddess, Demeter, was mourning the absence of her daughter, Persephone. Why did some women die in childbirth? It was the goddess Artemis shooting them with invisible arrows.

Many people think like this today about things that are not yet scientifically explained. For example, how do birds migrate so accurately? Why do certain cancers occur? These are often taken to be signs of the supernatural.

Gods and goddesses as humans

An easy way for the early Greeks to imagine powerful forces was to compare them with the most powerful people of the time—aristocratic rulers. They were nearly always male. So the chief divinity, Zeus, was seen as father Zeus.

Early Greek rulers liked to live in a palace on a hilltop, the safest place from which they could look down on their subjects. So Zeus, the sky god, was believed to rule from a palace on top of the towering and mysterious Mount Olympos, among the clouds. Human aristocrats were often tall, the result of having the best food and the pick of well-bred women to marry. So divinities were seen as tall too. Statues more than 40 feet (12 m) high were made of Zeus and Athena, his daughter.

In their palace on Olympos gods and goddesses enjoyed laughter, drink, and feasting—just as human rulers did. Human rulers enjoyed love affairs with women of lower status. So too did male gods. Zeus and his handsome son Apollo had many affairs with mortal women. Goddesses had far less freedom in

◀ Zeus, ruler of heaven and dispenser of justice. Here he seems sterner than the fun-loving Zeus portrayed in the *Iliad*, in which he is captivated by his wife, Hera, with her perfume and earrings.

▶ The great statue of Athena that stood in the Parthenon is now lost (see page 77). Its gold and ivory were probably looted. This is a small copy of the statue, made in Roman times.

love, again a reflection of real life. A noblewoman who loved a poor man would be disgraced.

While Greek aristocrats hoped that the gods, too, were aristocrats—only more powerful—many ordinary Greeks prayed that the gods would not behave like aristocrats. Hesiod, poet and farmer, imagined Zeus defending poor people against aristocratic injustice.

The philosopher Xenophanes protested against the idea that Zeus was an aristocratic, man-shaped being. He said that god was "in no way like mortals, in body or in thought." Poets were wrong, he claimed, to show gods cheating, stealing, and having love affairs. Ordinary Greeks in the classical period still believed in Zeus as a sky god, the lord of the lightning. But, they thought, he used his lightning to protect the weak by striking down the wicked.

▲ Poseidon, god of the sea and the earthquake—two very important things in Greece. The trident, the badge of a fisherman, shows his identity.

◀ The beautiful goddess of the moon, Artemis, as she draws her bow. She was also a huntress living in forests with the animals. Unlike her twin, Apollo, she was a virgin.

The Oracle at Delphi

PEOPLE ANXIOUS ABOUT THE FUTURE HAVE often turned to magic. Some people today look in astrology sections of newspapers to read what the future has in store for them, even if they claim not to believe in astrology! Ancient Greeks asked their gods. In return for a fee given to the priests, Zeus or Apollo would tell the future.

The oracle most famous for prophecy was at Delphi, far up in the mountains of central Greece, with views over distant valleys and the sea. The other two famous oracles were even farther away from the main Greek cities. One was at Dodone far to the northwest, and the other was in the North African desert. At Dodone, the god spoke in the rustlings of a very old oak tree, held sacred to Zeus. Greeks had long believed that gods lived far away and high up, on Mount Olympos and in the heavens. So the remote and lofty setting of Delphi made it a likely place for the supernatural.

How the oracle responded

Ordinary poor Greeks could get help at Delphi for a small fee. Records from Dodone show the sort of questions they must have asked. Shall I become a fisherman? Should I keep sheep? Did my servant steal the cloth? Should I marry? Am I the father of the baby my wife is carrying? Such questions had a simple answer: yes or no.

When a city asked a question at Delphi, it probably had to pay far more. The shrine often had to give a detailed answer, and if the answer was later proved to be wrong, the god at the shrine would lose his reputation—and the priests would lose business. So Delphi became famous for giving answers that had two or more possible meanings.

When the great Persian invasion was on its way, Delphi advised the Athenians to evacuate their city. This was good advice, and the Athenians followed it. But the shrine also prophesied that for the Athenians only a "wooden wall" would survive.

What did this mean? Was it the warships of Athens? They, of course, were made of wood. Or did the phrase mean a stockade of wood? This doubt protected the reputation of the shrine. If the Athenians had trusted their fleet and been defeated, the Delphians could claim that "wooden wall" had not meant ships after all.

The god who prophesied at Delphi was Apollo. His words were delivered by the lips of a priestess, the Pythia. But who was it that really prepared the prophecy? Much of it was cleverly expressed in complicated verse, which was helpful but also deliberately vague at times. The Pythia was said to be uneducated. Did she make it up? This was a question that the Delphians liked to keep mysterious. The words were the god's alone!

◀ Delphi—a remote place in the mountains where a god spoke to humans. The ruins of Apollo's temple can be seen in the foreground, including columns that once supported the roof.

▲ The Pythia, priestess of Apollo, utters a prophecy. She is seated on a sacred tripod. If she really helped make up Delphic prophecies, she was the most influential woman in the whole of Greece.

Olympia, Site of the Games

AT OLYMPIA, IN THE NORTHWESTERN Peloponnese (which should not be confused with Mount Olympos—see pages 66–67), was the most famous shrine of Zeus. It lay at the junction of two rivers, on a plain that was flat enough to be suitable for athletics.

Olympia was part of the territory of Elis, which was never a very powerful state. This encouraged other states to send treasures to the shrine and to add to its prestige—in helping Elis they were not helping a potential rival. Olympia became a showplace for the Greek world, used for both religious and political purposes. Olympia had been settled by Greeks of the Mycenaean age, but it was the Olympic Games that made the place famous.

The temple and statue of Zeus

A small hill on the site was named after Zeus's father, Kronos. Close to it, in the 400s B.C.E., was built the main temple in Zeus's honor. Soon after it was built, the people of Elis learned of the new statue of Athena, which Pheidias had made of gold and ivory at Athens (see page 77). They wanted one too— of Zeus. So Pheidias was hired, and duly made a towering statue to go inside the Olympian temple. Traces of his workshop have been found recently at Olympia. There is a cup that bears the words "I belong to Pheidias."

The origin of the Games

The Olympic Games were held at Olympia every four years (see pages 72–73). They were a religious event, sacred to Zeus. But, as is occasionally the case in today's Olympics, there were some unholy motives at work. Some of the sculpture on the temple of Zeus reflected the ferocious competition for which Olympia was known. This showed a chariot race from myth which, some said, was the contest from which the Games sprang.

Oinomaos, king of a nearby town, had a daughter named Hippodameia. He said that he would give her in marriage only to a man who could defeat him in a chariot race. But every suitor who lost a race was killed by the king with a spear in the back. His head was then cut off and put on display. Since the king's horses had supernatural powers, the killing of young men was likely to go on for some time.

However, Hippodameia fell in love with one of the suitors—Pelops. So she arranged for her father's chariot to be sabotaged. The sculpture on the temple of Zeus showed Oinomaos and Pelops just before the

◀ Olympic victors were able to increase their fame by dedicating treasure to Zeus at Olympia. This golden bowl, made around 600 B.C.E., bears the names of the sons of the tyrant of Corinth.

start of their race, in which the king's axle broke and he was killed by his competitor. Parts of the sculpture survive in the museum at Olympia. The columns of the temple that once supported it now lie collapsed in sections, brought down by an earthquake 1,000 years after they were built.

Because the Games drew crowds from all over the Greek world, Olympia was used for display. Victorious athletes put up statues to commemorate themselves. Different cities had their own treasuries at Olympia to advertise their successes—not all of them at athletics. Athens, for example, reminded people of its victory at the battle of Marathon, by putting on show, or "dedicating," the helmet of Miltiades, the commander of the victorious troops. (By a great piece of luck it has survived and is in the museum at Olympia.) After conquering most of Greece, in the 330s B.C.E., Philip of Macedon (father of Alexander) erected a building at Olympia to house statues of himself and his family.

▶ Violent stories were recalled in sculpture on the temple of Zeus at Olympia. Here a drunken centaur, soon to be killed, drags a beautiful woman away from a wedding.

▼ Plan of Olympia. The stadium (right) was the place for foot races. The palaestra (left) was the wrestling ground, and the scene of many murky deeds (see page 72).

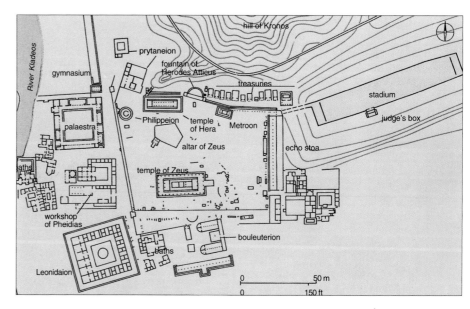

▶ Collapsed sections of columns from the temple of Zeus. They show how the drums of stone were held together by a piece of metal in the hole at the center of each.

▼ Olympia (center) lies on a site that is flat, green, and lush by Greek standards. Left is the wooded hill of Kronos. To the right, by the river, was the wrestling ground, or palaestra.

The Ancient Olympic Games

THE GREEK WORLD WAS MADE UP OF countless independent little states, many of them divided by war or by the fear of war. There was no central government of Greece and no capital city. But once every four years hostilities were put aside and a special truce was made so that people could go safely to Olympia for the Games.

Competitors in the Olympic Games might come from as far away as the colonies in Gaul or southern Russia. But the rule was that they all had to be Greek-speaking and of Greek descent. Any Greek male could compete, but only rich aristocrats could afford the time to train and take part. Many of the competitors took part naked. Women were barred, even as spectators, although a story was told of one mother who disguised herself as a man and managed to see her son win his event.

The events

The Games were a test of manly skills and strength, and several of the events were of military origin. Throwing the javelin and the discus derived from throwing spears and stones in war. The competition in chariot racing derived from the use of war chariots. The wrestling and boxing events represented the most primitive forms of fighting. Boxers wore gloves that were like boot soles, and fighting continued when one boxer was down on the ground. In the ferocious *pankration* (all-in wrestling) referees found it difficult to stop competitors from biting their opponents and gouging their eyes.

The rewards

Victory at the Games did not bring a gold medal, merely a wreath of leaves. Yet competition was intense. Why? People today are sometimes sentimental about the ancient Olympics, saying that the Greeks took part purely for the love of sport. But that is far from true. The winners became stars in their own cities and were gazed at in public and invited to luxurious parties. A winner could marry the girl of his choice, someone from a powerful family with a large dowry. Sometimes he was freed from taxation, and a city-state could give the equivalent of U.S. $500,000 to a victor. In other words, winning at Olympia brought riches and—most important—prestige and influence.

If a city's athletes won many victories at the Games, other Greeks might expect the men of that city to be hard in battle. If a city won the expensive horse racing or chariot racing, outsiders would assume that the city had the wealth necessary for war. So, although they brought a truce, the Games also carried warlike propaganda.

Cheating and punishment

With so much at stake, it is not surprising that many competitors cheated. If caught, they were punished. Anyone who gouged or bit, or tried to bribe the referee, had to set up a statue in bronze to Zeus, on which his name would be inscribed. This brought expense and disgrace—the exact opposite of what the competitors had entered the Games for.

▼ Competitors in four of the main Olympic events. Other events, such as mule-cart racing, brought less prestige. Notice the weights in the hands of the long jumper. In all these contests the competitors were naked.

Main events

Long jump *Javelin* *Discus* *Wrestling*

◄ A bronze statue of a boy jockey and victorious racehorse. It was the owners, rather than the jockeys and charioteers, who received all the glory from the horse events at Olympia.

◄ This young man is exercising with the special weights that were used in the long jump. They were carefully shaped to help the jumper balance.

▼ The starting line at the stadium, home of the most famous sprint in Greece. Notice the grooves cut in the stone that were to prevent the sprinters' feet from slipping.

▼ The arched entrance to the stadium at Olympia. Like the tunnel in a modern arena, it allowed the athletes to make a dramatic appearance.

◄ Two naked men brawl, as they would at Olympia in the *pankration*. The *pankration* combined wrestling and boxing.

City of Athens

WHEN THE DEFEATED PERSIAN INVADERS left Athens in 479 B.C.E., they vented their anger on its buildings. The Athenians, who had been refugees for a year, returned. Most of them were living in poverty. They found their homes and public buildings wrecked. Yet within 50 years the city became the jewel of the Mediterranean, glittering with marble temples and metal statues. How was the reconstruction done?

Rebuilding the city wall

Firstly, Athens needed a great circular wall to defend it against future invasion. Children and women joined the men and they all worked at desperate speed. Together, they managed to build the wall before suspicious Spartans could bring an army to prevent it. Thucydides, the historian of Athens, wrote that even ornamental stonework was seized to make

▶ The temple of Victory, built in the late fifth century B.C.E. Far smaller than the Parthenon, it stands by the Propylaia—the elaborate gateway to the Akropolis of Athens.

▼ The Akropolis and its surroundings at the heart of ancient Athens. The plan shows buildings from several periods. Close to the Akropolis are the Pnyx (where the assembly met), the theater of Dionysos, and the murder court, the Areiopagos.

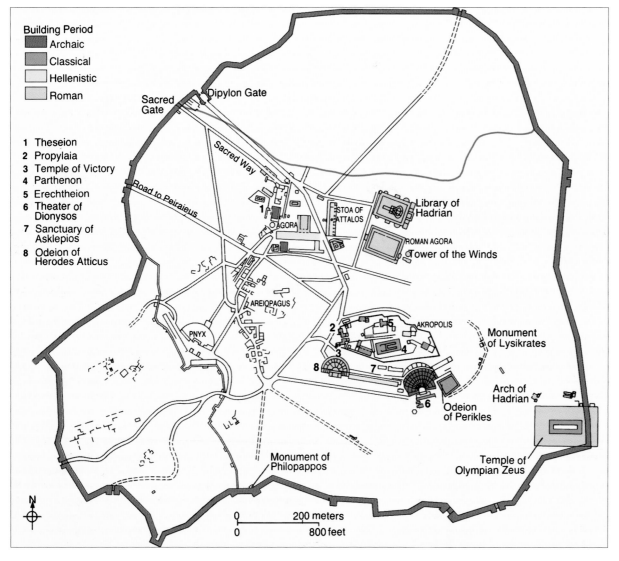

Building Period
- Archaic
- Classical
- Hellenistic
- Roman

1 Theseion
2 Propylaia
3 Temple of Victory
4 Parthenon
5 Erechtheion
6 Theater of Dionysos
7 Sanctuary of Asklepios
8 Odeion of Herodes Atticus

Sacred Gate
Dipylon Gate
Sacred Way
Road to Peiraieus
AGORA
STOA OF ATTALOS
Library of Hadrian
ROMAN AGORA
Tower of the Winds
AREIOPAGUS
PNYX
AKROPOLIS
Monument of Lysikrates
Arch of Hadrian
Odeion of Perikles
Temple of Olympian Zeus
Monument of Philopappos

0   200 meters
0   800 feet

N

▼ Athena, patron goddess of wisdom and war, and protector of the city of Athens. She was born by springing fully formed—and armed—from the head of her father, Zeus.

the wall. Archaeologists digging along the wall have found some of it, proving the truth of this.

Themistokles, one of Athens' cleverest politicians, tricked the Spartans into delaying their invasion until after the wall was built. However, he would have preferred the Athenians to build their new city not at Athens but at the port of Peiraieus located about 5 miles (8 km) away. He knew that the Athenians' great power was their fleet. Also, much of their food was brought in by sea. He was afraid that one day an invading army would encircle Athens and cut it off from the sea. If the Athenians would move their homes to the port, he believed they would be free from that danger.

The "long walls" to Peiraieus

The people of Athens would not leave the Akropolis, their great friendly rock, however, because they had grown up near it. It was very important to them. They had climbed it to take part in enjoyable festivals. And on top of the rock was the holiest shrine of Athena, the city's patron goddess.

So they stayed at Athens and found another way to prevent the city from being cut off. They built a wall to defend Peiraieus, then, in the early 450s B.C.E., a pair of roughly parallel long walls between Peiraieus and Athens. This corridor meant that Athenians and their goods could travel safely between the port and the city.

The Akropolis: symbol of power

In the early 440s B.C.E. the beautification of the Akropolis began (see pages 76–77). The burned ruins left by the Persians were cleared away. The centerpiece of the new buildings was a temple of marble for Athena, called the Parthenon. It was built so well that much of it is still in place, more than 2,500 years later. After the Parthenon was completed in 432 B.C.E., Greeks traveled to Athens to see it, as people do today from all parts of the world.

To other Greeks, Athens' expensive buildings suggested power. If Athens had so much money for fine architecture, how much must it have for war? The buildings were propaganda for Athens' empire. They also helped make Athens an attractive place for Greek visitors. Anaxagoras, who understood eclipses before other Greeks, came to stay at Athens. Aristotle, one of the world's greatest thinkers, came to study in Athens at Plato's Academy. They and many other distinguished immigrants appreciated the sheer beauty of the rebuilt city.

▲ The Propylaia (gateway) on the Akropolis, begun in 437 B.C.E. The temple of Victory is at top right. No other city spent so much money on a gateway.

▼ The Parthenon's roof was lost in an explosion of gunpowder in 1687. When new, the shining marble was seen from afar. The Parthenon was called "Athens' pretty face."

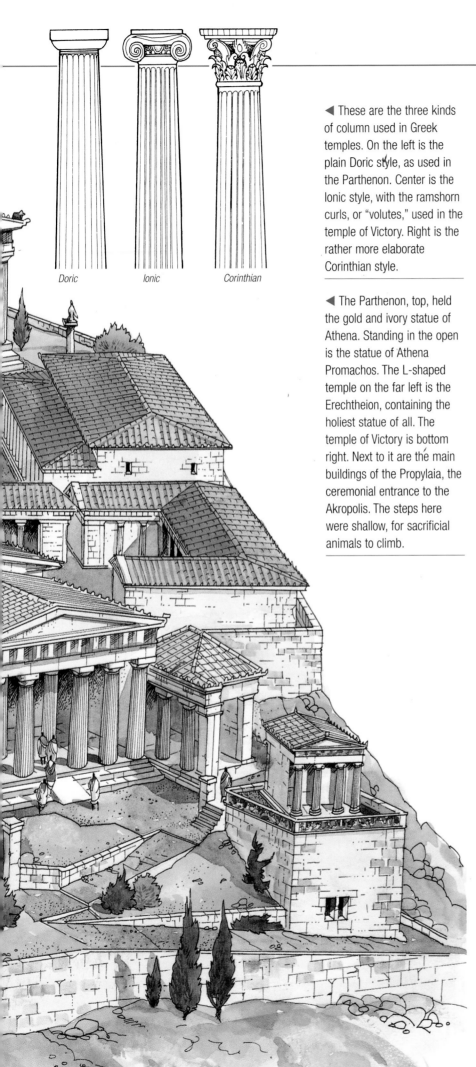

Doric   Ionic   Corinthian

◀ These are the three kinds of column used in Greek temples. On the left is the plain Doric style, as used in the Parthenon. Center is the Ionic style, with the ramshorn curls, or "volutes," used in the temple of Victory. Right is the rather more elaborate Corinthian style.

◀ The Parthenon, top, held the gold and ivory statue of Athena. Standing in the open is the statue of Athena Promachos. The L-shaped temple on the far left is the Erechtheion, containing the holiest statue of all. The temple of Victory is bottom right. Next to it are the main buildings of the Propylaia, the ceremonial entrance to the Akropolis. The steps here were shallow, for sacrificial animals to climb.

THE AKROPOLIS, THE "HIGH CITY" OF Athens, was chosen as the site for fine temples. The goddess Athena was thought to deserve this lofty position of honor, with the best views, for her houses.

The Akropolis also made a wonderful setting for the outdoor festivals of the Athenians. Children and women joined the men, all showing off their best clothes. Animals for sacrifice climbed the Akropolis and everyone had free meat—a luxury in a country where there was little land suitable for grazing and animals were scarce.

Opposition to the new building

The Parthenon was built of local marble from Mount Pendeli and was the largest building on the Akropolis. But many other elegant structures were built there at the same period, from 450 to 404 B.C.E. Some conservative politicians opposed this big project. They said that the Parthenon made Athens look like "a deceitful woman." They meant that the new temple was brilliant white, with small brightly painted sections. Women often put on white make-up, with dabs of rouge, hoping to look richer than they really were. (Wealthy women stayed indoors most of the time, which kept them pale.)

The real reason these politicians opposed the building scheme was that they wanted to put up public buildings at their own expense, so that they would get the credit and people would give them political support. But the buildings on the Akropolis were financed by income from Athens' empire—the people's empire. Despite the opposition, the great building project on the Akropolis went ahead. It involved a large number of sculptors, masons, painters, and other craftsmen.

The statue of Athena

The Parthenon did not house a crowd of worshipers, as churches do. Worshipers sacrificed outside. Inside was a towering statue of the warrior goddess. Athena's armor was made of gold, her flesh of ivory—for whiteness and to show her femininity.

The most sacred statue of all was old and simple, roughly made from wood. In order to house it, the new Erechtheion was built. Named after a legendary king of Athens—Erechtheus—the building featured female figures as supports (see page 5). In the open was the statue of Athena Promachos ("the defender"). It could be seen gleaming in the distance by sailors from many miles away.

Sculptures of the Parthenon

OWADAYS THE STONEWORK OF MANY ruined temples has a faded dignified color. But when the temples were new they looked very different. The freshly cut stone of the columns was a brilliant white. And sculpture on the temples was painted in strong colors, such as red and blue.

In the decades before the Parthenon was built, Greek sculptors had learned to carve animal and human forms accurately. Pheidias, who directed the work on the Parthenon, was one of the greatest of all Greek artists.

The masterpieces of Pheidias

Pheidias and his men carved a frieze out of Athenian marble—a series of scenes to run along all four sides of the Parthenon's interior. It showed a procession held every four years to honor Athena. The procession was known as the Great Panathenaia.

Young men are portrayed showing off their wealth as they did in real life by driving chariots in the procession. Some of the horses are galloping, their manes flying out behind them. Girls carry sacred water for the goddess, and an incense burner. One young person is shown carrying a new robe for the goddess. (Every four years the garment on her old wooden statue had to be changed.) Cattle are being dragged to sacrifice, one animal resisting and throwing up its head. A rope restrains the animal,

▼ Handsome young men of Athens gallop in procession. Notice the horses' flying manes and, in the nostril and cheek of the horse on the right, the drill holes that once held a bronze bridle.

but today this has to be imagined. It was painted on the sculpture, and now the paint has gone.

Another sculpture on the temple showed a nasty episode from myth. A group of centaurs, part-human, part-horse, had been invited to a wedding. Getting drunk, they had seized the bride and tried to carry her off. The sculpture shows the resulting battle between centaurs and men. Centaurs may have reminded people of "barbarous" Persians, and of their defeat by civilized Greeks.

More famous in his own time, however, was Pheidias's gold-and-ivory statue of Athena (see pages 67 and 77). The statue was immense—about 40 feet (12 m) high. Pheidias, afraid someone would accuse him of stealing part of the gold, made the gold on the statue detachable. Then people could take it off and check its weight.

The surviving sculptures

Many of the stone sculptures from the Parthenon can be seen today in the British Museum in London. Greece would like them to be returned to Athens, where they could be displayed in a new museum on the Akropolis. The sculptures were originally brought to London by the earl of Elgin and sold to the British Museum in 1816. They are known as the Elgin Marbles. Where they should now be displayed remains a matter of controversy.

▶ In Pheidias's workshop. A sculptor chisels the figure of a horse from a block of local marble. The projecting lumps of stone will be used to attach ropes when the sculpture is hoisted into place. The T-shaped holes are for pieces of metal to hold the stonework together.

▼ Left: The struggle to control a cow led to its sacrifice. Right: A drunken centaur uses his horse's leg to pin down a man, while with his human arm he prepares to stab him.

Painting on Pottery

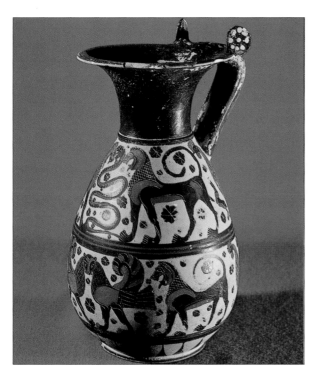

▲ A very early Geometric vase from the Greek dark age, soon after 1000 B.C.E. The pattern of wavy lines is derived from the art of the even earlier Mycenaean civilization. There is no representation yet of the human figure.

P ICTURES ON POTTERY ARE SOME OF THE best-looking things that have survived from ancient Greece. They are also useful to us because the provide information on how things would have looked in the Greek world. This is why many of them, and especially the Red Figure vase-paintings from Athens, have been reproduced in the pages of this book.

Mycenaean and Geometric styles

Styles of vase-painting differed from place to place and from one period to another. After the fall of Mycenae, designs were for a long time very simple, sometimes using the wavy-line patterns the Mycenaeans had been fond of. Then, not long before 1000 B.C.E., the Geometric style came in, using far more complex patterns. Simple pictures of men and women appeared among the patterns, almost as "matchstick men" but with broad shoulders and very narrow waists, still in the Mycenaean style.

▲ A seventh-century B.C.E. Corinthian vase, with a design inspired by contacts with Africa and the east. Notice the African lions and the imaginary beast that appears to be part-panther, part-bird.

▼ A complex Athenian design dating from the eighth century B.C.E., with zigzags and meandering lines. Other Geometric vases at this time showed human and animal figures in simple scenes.

The display of wealth and status

Two specialist craftsmen were usually needed for the making of a fine pot—the potter and the painter. The work was done by hand, and so the best-painted vases were expensive. Since wealthy men were the main buyers, the paintings often showed things that had a particular appeal to the rich. For example, Geometric vases sometimes showed elaborate funerals. These involved big processions and were a favorite way for wealthy families to show off their supporters and their power.

The horse is often seen in Geometric art. An expensive horse, like an expensive car today, was a regular way of showing off.

In the seventh and sixth centuries B.C.E., artists in Corinth painted more elaborate figures, often of real or imaginary animals—with eastern and African connections. Lions and sphinxes, for example, reminded some Corinthians that they had grown wealthy from trade with Egypt.

Black Figure and Red Figure styles

The most famous styles of vase-painting are from Athens: the Black Figure (on a red background) dates mainly from the sixth century B.C.E., and the Red Figure (on a black background) is mainly from the fifth century B.C.E.

Both colors were made from the same clay, but the clay was differently treated in the kiln to produce the two types. Because color pigments were few and

▶ The design from an Athenian Black Figure cup of the mid-sixth century B.C.E. Herakles, commonly identified by his lion-skin cap, wrestles with the sea god Triton. Care has been taken to show variety in each of the dresses of the ring of dancers.

the spaces for painting on pottery were small, there was not much scope for detail. Artists therefore carefully chose symbols that would help people understand the pictures. In the large picture below, the fish in the inner circle indicate that one of the wrestlers is a sea god.

The paintings often matched the use of the pot. The wrestling scene is from a wine cup, designed for parties. Wine cups often depict scenes of aggression because drink made men have violent fantasies. They also show pictures of women dancers who would perform at parties.

◀ Making a vase at Athens. The work was done by both men and women. The separate processes of shaping the pot and painting it were usually done by different people.

Everyday Life in Athens

ATHENS IN ITS GREAT DAYS (FROM THE FIFTH to the fourth centuries B.C.E.) was probably the most colorful city of the Mediterranean world. Travelers from remote Greek cities and from the Persian Empire brought news, ideas, and things to sell. Athenian children in the great port of Peiraieus would have heard sailors speaking in different languages. Street behavior was generally respectful, often noisy, but sometimes violent.

Life in the streets

A simple Athenian man awoke at dawn, scratching himself from insect bites. The walls of his room were of mud-brick. (A burglar in Greek was called a "wall digger." Burrowing into a house was obviously quite easy.) He then set off to do the shopping, which, in Greece, was men's work.

On his way to market our man would see slaves and the very poor with large burdens on their backs, and women carrying great pitchers of water. Few houses had their own water supply; most people had to visit a spring. He would carefully avoid the slops and mess that had been dumped overnight in the unlit streets—Athens had no sewer system. He might catch a glimpse of a woman or a girl peeping out from an expensive house, but as soon as she saw him she would disappear, out of pride. Boys were far more a part of street life than girls. Boys worked as soon as they were able, and the sons of better-off parents walked through the streets to school.

At night the streets became dangerous. Thieves specialized in attacking travelers in the dark. Some men carried blazing torches as a weapon as well as for light. Young men, drunk after parties, roamed the dark streets, battering at the doors of women.

Behavior of citizens

Market traders were generally looked down on and had to be protected by law from insult. Athens was famous for its freedom of speech, however. Poor men

▼ An Athenian street. For lack of even simple machinery, Greeks carried many burdens on their own backs. In Athens rich and poor mingled easily. In the streets of other cities, rich men swept the poor aside. Women escorted each other, ignoring the stares of men.

and some slaves stood up for themselves and would not always allow themselves to be intimidated by the rich. One rich man complained that at Athens even horses and donkeys seemed to be full of self-confidence as they walked along.

Ordinary people argued and joked in the market about the price of favorite Athenian foods, such as eels and salted fish, honey, and game birds. They might not have taken much notice of small groups of wealthy men strolling along in white robes, talking about politics or religion. If they did, they might not have approved of them, since many of these political theorists and philosophers, such as Thucydides, Kritias, and Plato, despised ordinary Athenians and disliked the power that democracy gave them. Rich intellectuals thought that ordinary citizens were too uneducated to run the city's affairs and that they themselves should be in charge. Poorer citizens of course resented this attitude, and sometimes punished a leading antidemocrat.

▶ A Greek barber at work. Barbers' shops were favorite places for meeting and gossiping, like "a party without wine," as one writer described them.

▶ Although made in southern Italy, this vase shows an everyday scene in Athens—a fishmonger at work. Notice the fish's head on the floor.

▶ Man plowing with oxen. Most Athenians were, in fact, country-dwellers. Only occasionally did they crowd into the city—for shopping or festivals, or for protection during wartime.

Spartan Life

DAILY LIFE IN SPARTA WAS VERY DIFFERENT from that of Athens. Sparta was like an army camp. Men and boys prepared constantly for the need to fight helots and other enemies. For young Spartans, life was competitive and savage.

Boys trained as fighters

Spartan boys were forced to become tough. They had to walk barefoot. Even in cold weather they could only wear one cloak. They were kept hungry and told to steal food, but if they were caught stealing they were beaten—to teach them to steal more skillfully in future. There was even a stealing competition. Boys had to steal pieces of cheese while trying to dodge blows from whips. The whip, used by older boys on younger ones, was an important part of Spartan upbringing.

This education in hardship was probably meant to teach young Spartan men how to hunt runaway helots. Helot-hunting would mean sneaking undetected around the countryside and living off stolen food. If a helot was caught traveling at night, he would be killed.

Strength and courage were also necessary qualities in hoplite battles against Sparta's enemies from other states. Spartan boys learned to fear the authority of their elders and to do what they were told. Armies down through the ages have taught that orders must be obeyed immediately. On the battlefield there is no time for any argument. In Sparta itself older people were given more power and respect than in any other Greek city.

Fear of family life

In Sparta, boys may have had to sleep together rather than returning to their families at night. Young married couples were not allowed to be seen together and would meet secretly at night. Man and wife were not meant to become close companions. Men of all ages had to have evening meals together in military messes, away from their women.

Sparta feared the family. Differences, from being brought up in separate families, can make people dislike one another. Loyalty to one's own family can lead to feuds between families. That was the last thing Sparta wanted. If Sparta was weakened by quarrels, helots and other enemies would have a chance to attack. So Spartan boys were educated, away from the family, to be loyal to the whole community. Spartan citizens were called the *homoioi*, which meant "the men who are similar."

▶ This sinister warrior in bronze is probably Spartan. Notice the long hair, in the Spartan style, reaching far below his helmet. The sight of such Spartans would have caused people to be afraid.

Scorning weakness

Other Greek cities, including Athens, had relaxed and happy times at religious festivals, when people drank much wine. Mass drunkenness was common. If the Spartans had been allowed to do this, the helots would have had a wonderful chance to revolt. But in Sparta heavy drinking by citizens was banned. Instead, a few helots were deliberately made to get very drunk while young Spartans were brought to watch their stupid doings. In this way the young learned to despise drunkenness.

Sparta often used humiliation as a way of teaching its young citizens. A man who failed to fight bravely in battle was called a "trembler." He was made to shave one side of his face and grow a beard on the other, so that everyone would pick on him and laugh at him. He was forbidden to look happy and he was ignored when teams were selected for ball games.

The Spartans, who were outnumbered by the helots, were always anxious to breed more citizens. Therefore, men who did not marry were forced to strip naked once a year and walk in a public procession. Spartan girls were brought to watch and shout cruel things at them. That, they thought, would teach men to marry!

Spartan girls were granted more freedom than was usual for Greek city-states. They were able to walk about freely. They also received an education, could own property, and managed farms while the men were away fighting (see page 87).

▼ Spartan boys playing a rough game. Spartans were taught to look on the bright side of death. A brave death in battle was a source of pride to relatives. The bodies and graves of brave men were displayed to make young people feel at ease with the sight. If a king died far away in war, his body was brought home preserved in honey for burial in Sparta.

The Secluded World of Women

WOMEN AND GIRLS OF WEALTHY families lived quite apart from men. They seldom spoke to males, even their male relatives. The men spent their days outdoors in the sunlight, while the women and their daughters were confined to their home. On special family occasions they were allowed out—to see a baby born or attend a funeral. If a young woman of wealthy family did go out often, her husband would be told by other men to guard his wife "with bolts and watchful slaves."

Why were women controlled like this? A Greek man dreaded that his wife or daughter would find a lover. If she did, no one could be sure who was the father of her children. The children would not be allowed to become citizens. This would disgrace the whole family. Only citizens were able to own land or defend their aged parents in the law courts.

Life for Athenian women

Staying at home, prosperous women supervised their slaves. The slaves did most of the housework and raised the small children of the family. Some women could read and enjoyed reading, or watching, the sophisticated tragic drama of Athens.

Girls did not go to school, however, and probably most of them were illiterate. Some men thought that females definitely should not be allowed to read. They worried that they would learn too much and then argue with their husbands!

▶ The goddess Athena who seems here to be mourning by a gravestone. Women died on average about 10 years earlier than men—in their mid-30s. Childbirth was often the cause of death.

Poor women, on the other hand, could not afford to stay indoors. They went out to work, either fetching water, selling in the market, or picking fruit. Some of them were employed as wet nurses, which means that they suckled other people's babies. Being outdoors often, girls from poor families would meet young men and might marry for love. (The daughters of the rich were not supposed to know any men, and their marriages were arranged by their parents.)

Women who entertained

Very poor young women and slaves, if they had the good fortune to be pretty and clever, often learned to play music, to dance, and to entertain men at parties. These entertainers were called *hetairai*. But the parties they went to were rough and disreputable. After drinking heavily the men were often on their worst behavior. A wealthy woman usually looked down on the *hetairai*—she was proud

▲ Two young women seen in private conversation, in a charming and very lifelike terra-cotta piece from the late classical period.

▶ *Hetairai* danced, played music and performed sexually for men at noisy parties. But while the men drank wine, the women stayed sober.

hardship, pain, and the risk of death. Childbirth meant the same things for a woman. The only Spartans to be honored with marked tombs were men who had been killed in battle and women who had died in childbirth.

In spite of being tough, Spartan women never acted as soldiers. When an enemy force approached Sparta in 370 B.C.E., the women panicked. They caused more noise and confusion than the enemy, according to Aristotle.

Women in other cities were different. We hear of women in Kerkyra (Corfu) and Plataia (see page 35) taking part in street fighting. They stood on rooftops yelling and throwing heavy tiles at the enemy.

▲ The rolling of dough in a bakery, work usually done by slave women. If done by a citizen, both she and her family might be cruelly teased for their poverty.

▶ The kitchen of prosperous Athenians. In the background a woman is weaving—clothes were usually made at home. The woman mixing food has the short hair of a slave.

of living among respected women, albeit in a shadowy world of their own. But some *hetairai* became women of distinction.

Sappho and Thargelia

Greek cities of the eastern Aegean gave more freedom to women. Sappho, a noblewoman of Lesbos, for example, learned to write fine poetry. She wrote about her girlfriends, sometimes lovingly, but sometimes jealously and cattily. Only fragments of her poems survive, including the lines "Some say that a troop of cavalry is the most lovely sight on earth, some say that hoplites are, or some say ships of war, but I say it is the person you love."

Thargelia from Miletos understood politics and became an agent of the king of Persia. It was her job to become the lover of powerful Greek men and then persuade them to support the Persians.

Spartan women

The citizen women of Sparta left their housework to helot women and learned to run and wrestle like men. This physical training was meant to make them fit and strong for childbirth. Not only would they cope better with the pain and stress of childbearing, but it was thought that strong, muscular women would produce tough children.

Spartans saw childbirth as the female equivalent of a battle. Battle for a Spartan man involved

Entertainment at the Theater

DRAMA WAS ONE OF THE GREATEST inventions of the Greeks. The word "drama" meant action, and the action on stage usually took the form of tragedy or comedy.

In Athens, plays were performed as part of a religious festival in honor of Dionysos, the god of "wet nature"—which included wine. The audiences for comedies had probably drunk enough wine to produce an excited atmosphere.

Huge numbers of people came to the drama. The assembly for political decision-making contained about 6,000, but the theater held more than 10,000 spectators. So the dramatic festival was perhaps the time for the community of Athens to feel happy and united. Poor Athenians were given money so that they could afford theater tickets.

Whether women attended the drama is uncertain. But there is a story of women being present in the audience and being so frightened by what they saw that they gave birth prematurely.

Tragedy

What happened on stage was not violent. The characters wore masks, however, and in a tragedy these could be very frightening. There were only two or three actors—plus the chorus. The actors switched masks as they changed roles. They often told of violence offstage—for example, when King Agamemnon was murdered by his wife and his dying screams filled the theater.

▶ The quality of sound in an auditorium like this could be marvelous. Even today in the ancient theater at Epidauros, natural speech sounds as if it is being amplified by a microphone. The large semicircular space, known as the *orchestra*, was for the chorus to dance in.

▶ Comic slaves and servants were favorite figures in Athenian comedy. There are many comic figurines such as these, usually with grotesque masks and padded costumes, but very few tragic ones.

◀ Hideous masks allowed actors in Greek tragedy to impress and scare the audience. By swapping masks, one actor could quickly portray a number of different characters.

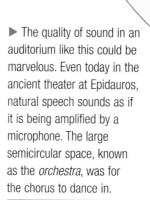

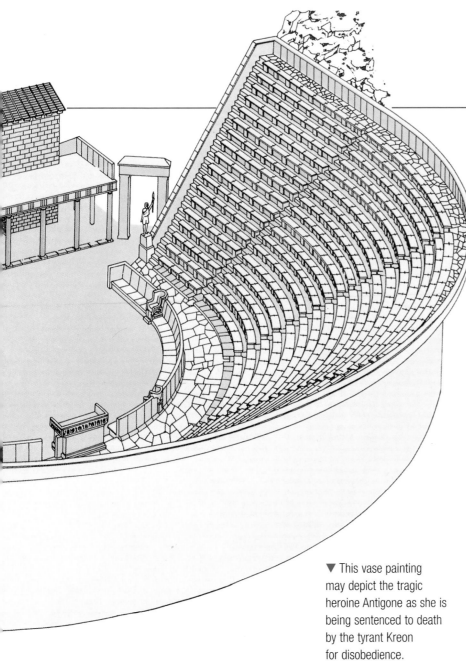

"How could I? I'm not using perfume."
"Can't a woman get a lover without perfume?"
"This one can't, unfortunately."

Comedy teased not only top people but also the gods. Dionysos himself was shown on stage being hit like a slave. A comic character complains to Zeus that the gods are allowing a terrible war to damage Athens. Zeus is then insulted by the character who rides up to heaven on a dung beetle.

In all, Aristophanes wrote some 30 plays, 11 of which have survived. Examples of later comedy by other playwrights have survived but they are not so directly political.

The importance of drama to Athens

Why was drama more popular in Athens than in other Greek cities? In tragedy the mythical characters who suffer are aristocrats. In comedy it is mainly the rich and famous who are mocked.

Athens was the leading democracy, where the poor, ordinary citizens had great power. Although they usually allowed the rich to survive and to have important positions in the city, the poor did feel some resentment toward them. Drama was a safe means of expressing this resentment. It allowed the poor for a moment to look down on aristocrats and the wealthy, either with pity or in mockery. In other cities the poor were not allowed to despise their leaders, even on stage.

▼ This vase painting may depict the tragic heroine Antigone as she is being sentenced to death by the tyrant Kreon for disobedience.

Tragedy was usually about events from the mythical past. Men and women who were partly good, partly bad, were shown coming to grief, often through a conflict between human action and divine law. The most famous authors of tragic plays were Aischylos, Sophokles, and Euripides.

In a play by Euripides, the noble young huntsman Hippolytos insults Aphrodite, goddess of love. She takes revenge by making Hippolytos' stepmother fall in love with him. When he refuses to be her lover, she causes his death in a chariot crash.

Comedy

Comedy was very often about life in contemporary Athens. Politicians and other famous people were teased, commonly about their love lives. Perikles, the great general and statesman, was accused in fun of being controlled by his girlfriend. In a comedy by Aristophanes, an ordinary citizen is shown asking his wife whether she has had a lover:

Houses at Olynthos

OLYNTHOS WAS A STRONG AND WEALTHY town near the coast of Chalkidike in northeastern Greece. It was close—too close, as it turned out—to Macedonia. In the 430s and 420s B.C.E. Olynthos was successful in leading a revolt against Athens—something that other powerful towns had tried and failed to do. But in 348 B.C.E. Olynthos was captured by Philip of Macedon (see pages 42–43). He could not tolerate the survival of a strong hostile town so close to Macedonia, and he therefore ordered the place to be demolished.

The demolition of Olynthos, like the later destruction of the Roman town of Pompeii, has proved to be a blessing for today's archaeologists. Most ancient towns were gradually changed and rebuilt, with remains of the older buildings being hacked about confusingly to make way for the foundations of newer ones. At Olynthos (and Pompeii) this did not happen. The foundations and ruined lower walls of the houses at Olynthos were left alone and give the best archaeological evidence of how Greeks built their homes.

House construction and design

Many houses at Olynthos were built on a regular grid of streets, with continuous foundations of rubble running from one house to the next. In one section houses were built in blocks of 10, with each block made up of two parallel rows of five houses. These houses were each 60 feet (18 m) wide and joined side to side. Walls were of sunbaked mud, and some of the floors were decorated with mosaics made of different-colored pebbles.

Greece, then as now, was baking hot for much of the year but had freezing weather in winter. Houses at Olynthos were designed to deal with this. They used a courtyard aligned with the sun. For use in the winter and at other cool times there was a sheltered balcony along three sides of the courtyard. It looked south, west, and east, allowing the family to sit in the sun at most times of the day. The roof over the balcony kept the summer sun from entering the upper rooms and overheating them. Beneath the balcony was a sheltered portico where in summer there would always be shade. (No doubt the balcony above the courtyard was used to dry clothes, as balconies often are in Greece today.)

In the middle of the courtyard was a small altar. There the family could make private sacrifices to the gods. They would ask the gods for prosperity, good health, and safety in wartime.

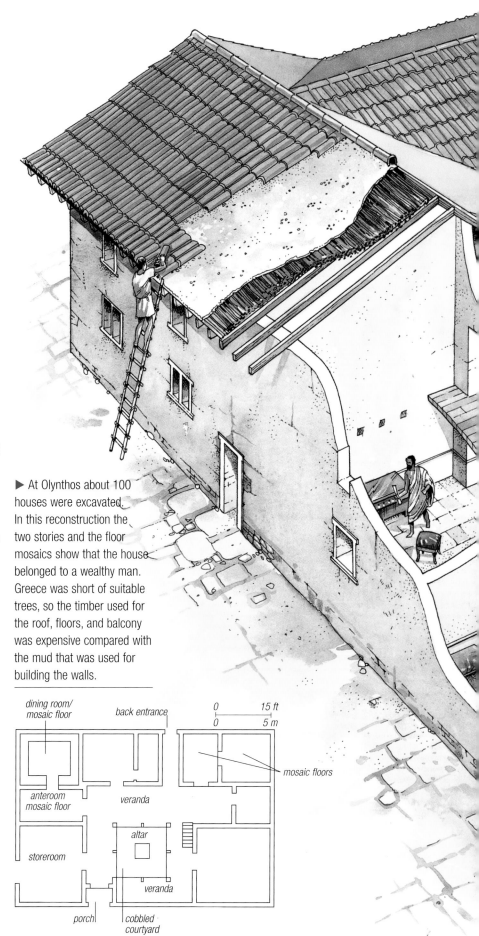

► At Olynthos about 100 houses were excavated. In this reconstruction the two stories and the floor mosaics show that the house belonged to a wealthy man. Greece was short of suitable trees, so the timber used for the roof, floors, and balcony was expensive compared with the mud that was used for building the walls.

dining room/ mosaic floor   back entrance   0 — 15 ft / 0 — 5 m

mosaic floors

anteroom mosaic floor   veranda

storeroom   altar

veranda

porch   cobbled courtyard

The enclosed courtyard

With high walls on all sides, the courtyard of an Olynthian house was completely private. This was intentional. Prosperous Greek men insisted that their women should be sheltered from the world of males and from any male stranger who entered the building (see pages 86–87.)

The lives of some women were so private that, after their deaths, outsiders had no sure way of telling that they had ever existed. The women's quarters in the Olynthian houses were almost certainly on the upper floor, as far as possible from the doors that led on to the street.

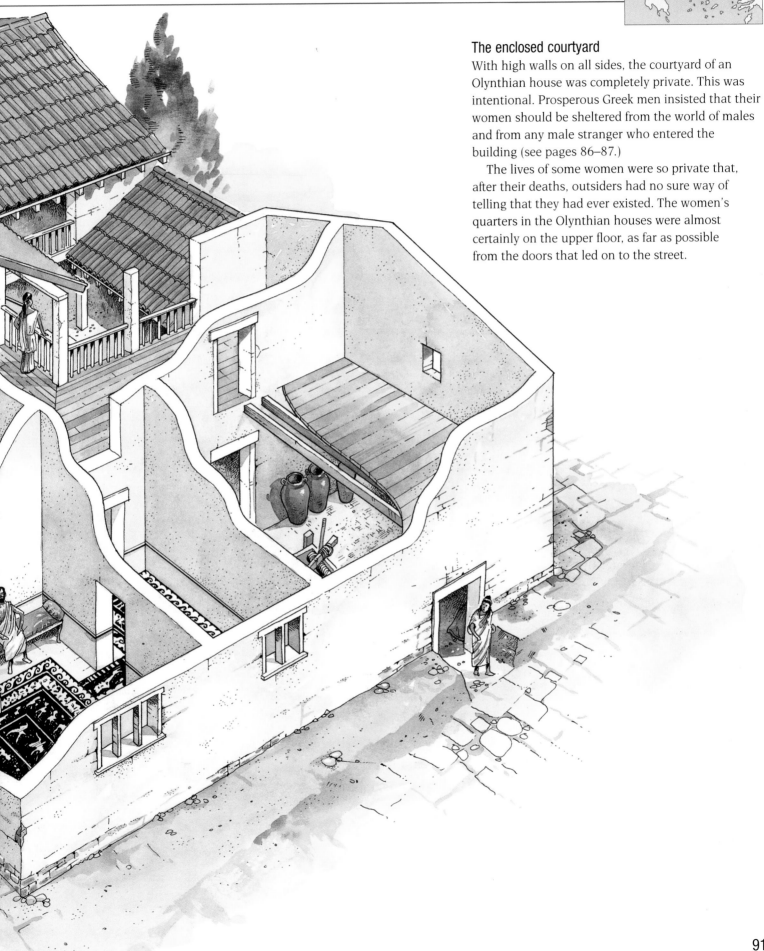

Glossary

akropolis "High city." A hill to which the citizens of a Greek town could retreat for defense. The most famous akropolis was at Athens.

archaic period The term now used for the time between the dark age and the classical period; roughly the 700s to the 480s B.C.E.

Attica The district surrounding and belonging to Athens. In its villages and towns lived most Athenian citizens.

Black Figure pottery This was made at Athens, especially in the sixth century B.C.E. The dark figures stood out against a reddish background.

centaur A creature of myth, with the head and torso of a man but the four legs and body of a horse.

citizenship To own land and take part in decision-making in a Greek state, it was necessary to be a citizen of the state. Citizenship was inherited. It was almost impossible for outsiders—Greek or foreign—to become citizens, though they might live there and be respected.

classical period The time between 480 B.C.E. and the age of Alexander (330s–320s B.C.E.).

Delian League The modern name given to an alliance of Greek states that was formed in 477 B.C.E. to carry on war against the Persians. Its headquarters was on the mid-Aegean island of Delos. The power of Athens turned the Delian League into an Athenian Empire.

demos The citizen body, and especially the mass of poor citizens in a Greek state.

demokratia (democracy) A form of government in which the supreme power belonged to mass meetings of the demos (people). Many Greek states had it, especially in the fifth century B.C.E. when the most famous democratic state, Athens, was at its zenith. The state most bitterly and actively opposed to demokratia was Sparta.

Hellenistic The name given to the Greek-speaking civilization that spread through many lands of the eastern Mediterranean and beyond following the conquests of Alexander the Great.

helots The mass of unfree citizens in Lakonia and Messenia, whose labor supported the Spartans. Fear of the helots turned the Spartans into a fiercely militaristic community.

homoioi ("the similars") The male citizens of Sparta who were deliberately educated alike so that they would have standardized personalities. Sparta had to be a harmonious community to resist its many enemies.

hoplites Infantrymen, armed with stabbing spears and round shields, who fought shoulder to shoulder, usually in a force that was several ranks deep.

Linear B The modern name for the script, composed of signs and pictures, in which Mycenaean Greeks kept records on tablets of clay.

millennium A period of 1,000 years. "The second millennium B.C.E." means the period from 2000 to 1000 B.C.E.

Minoan The name now given to the great civilization of Crete in the first half of the second millennium B.C.E. The word comes from the name of King Minos, a character of Greek legend who was remembered as having ruled in Crete before the Trojan War.

oligarchy Government of a Greek state by a few wealthy men. Oligarchs were of course strongly opposed to democracy.

ostracism An Athenian system of choosing between rival, highly influential politicians. Voters wrote on pieces of broken pot (ostraka), these being plentiful and valueless. The politician who received most votes against his name was ostracized—sent into exile for 10 years.

Peloponnese The large landmass that forms the southern part of mainland Greece.

phalanx The battle formation of hoplites, shoulder to shoulder and sometimes many ranks deep.

polis The Greek word for a self-governing Greek city, town, or village. From this word come many modern words, such as "politics," "policy," and "police."

Red Figure pottery This showed figures in red on a dark background. Such vases were produced at Athens from the late sixth century B.C.E. onwards.

trireme A long Greek warship with about 170 oars, arranged in three banks. Its main weapon was an underwater ram at its bow.

tyranny Government by one man whose will was above the law.

FURTHER READING

Books for young people
Hewitt, S. *The Greeks* (Franklin Watts, 1998).
MacDonald, F. *Gods & Goddesses: In the Daily Life of the Ancient Greeks* (Hodder Wayland, 2002).
MacDonald, F. *Inside Ancient Athens* (Enchanted Lion Books, 2005).
Pearson, A. *The Greeks* (Hodder Wayland, 1997).
Picard, B. L. *The Odyssey* (Oxford University Press, 2000).
Powell, A., and P. Steele. *The Greek News* (Walker Books, 1996).
Renault, M. *The Bull from the Sea* (Vintage, 2001).
Schlomp, V. *The Ancient Greeks* (Benchmark Books, 1996).
Sheehan, S. *Illustrated Encyclopaedia of Ancient Greece* (Getty Trust, 2002).

Reference books for adults
Beard, M., and J. Hendersen. *Classics: A Very Short Introduction* (Oxford University Press, 1995).
Boardman, J., Griffin, J., and O. Murray (eds.). *Oxford History of the Classical World* (Oxford University Press, 1986).
Burckhardt, J., et al. *The Greeks and Greek Civilization* (Fontana, 1999).
Cartledge, P. *Alexander the Great* (Pan Books, 2005).
Cartledge, P. (ed.). *Cambridge Illustrated History of Ancient Greece* (Cambridge University Press, 1998).
Cartledge, P. *The Greeks* (Oxford University Press, 1993).
Cartledge, P. *The Spartans* (Channel Four Books, 2002).

Dillon, M. *The Ancient Greeks in Their Own Words* (Sutton Publishing, 2002).
Hansen, V. D. *The Wars of the Ancient Greeks* (Cassell, 2001).
Powell, A. *Athens and Sparta* (Routledge, 1988).

Useful Web sites
http://www.ancientgreece.com
World News Web site with lots of information about the ancient Greeks.

http://www.bbc.co.uk/history/ancient/greeks/
British Broadcasting Corporation Web site includes features and links relating to ancient Greece.

http://www.historylink101.com/ancient_greece.htm
History Link 101's ancient Greece page connects you to pages about art, daily life, maps, pictures, and biographies.

http://library.thinkquest.org/10805/greece.html
Comprehensive site about ancient Greece.

http://www.museum.upenn.edu/greek_world/Index.html
University of Pennsylvania Museum of Archaeology and Anthropology Web site.

Gazetteer

The gazetteer lists places and features, such as islands or rivers, found on the maps. Each has a separate entry including a page and grid reference number. For example: Amantia 52 A3

All features are shown in italic type. For example: *Aoos, r.* 52 B3

A letter after the feature describes the kind of feature:
d. district; *i.* island; *isls.* islands; *r.* river

Abydos 57 D3
Acharnai 55 D4
Acheloos, r. 11 B3, 54 B4
Aegean Sea 11 D3, 58 B4
Aigina, i. 11 C2 , 55 D3
Aigospotamoi 57 D3
Akrotiri 11 D2
Aliakmon, r. 11 C4, 53 D3
Alos 53 D2
Alpheios, r. 11 B2, 55 C3
Amantia 52 A3
Ambracian Gulf 52 B1
Ambrakia 52 B2
Amnisos 54 G2
Amorgos, i. 11 D2, 59 B2
Amphilochian Argos 53 C1
Amphipolis 56 A3
Amphissa 55 C4
Amyklai 55 C3
Anaktorion 52 B1
Andros, i. 11 D2, 58 A3
Antandros 57 D2
Antigoneia 52 B3
Antissa 57 D2
Aoos, r. 52 B3
Apollonia 52 A3
Apollonia 57 E2
Arachthos, r. 52 B2
Argos 55 C3
Asine 11 C2, 55 C3
Askra 55 D4
Assos 57 D2
Athens 11 C2, 55 D3
Athos, Mount 11 D4
Attica, d. 11 C3
Aulis 55 D4
Axios, r. 53 D3

Bassai 54 B3
Belevi 59 D3

Black Sea 11 F4
Büyük Menderes, r. 59 D3

Chaironeia 55 C4
Chalkidike, d. 11 C4
Chalkis 11 C3, 55 D4
Chios 59 C4
Chios, i. 11 D3, 59 B4
Corinth 11 C2, 55 C3
Corinth, Gulf of 11 C3, 55 C4
Corinth, Isthmus of 55 C3
Crete, i. 11 D1, 54 F2
Crete, Sea of 11 D1, 54 F2
Cyclades, isls. 11 D2, 58 A3

Delos 58 B3
Delphi 11 C3, 55 C4
Didyma 59 D3
Dion 53 D3
Dodecanese, isls. 11 E2, 59 C2
Dodone 10 B3, 52 B2
Dyme 11 B3

Elataia 55 C4
Eleusis 11 C3, 55 D4
Elis 54 B3
Ephesos 59 D3
Epidamnos 52 A4
Epidauros 55 D3
Epirus, d. 10 B3
Eretria 55 D4
Erythrai 59 C4
Euboia, Gulf of 55 D4
Euboia, i. 11 C3, 55 E4
Euros, r. 11 E4
Eurotas, r. 55 C3

Gla 11 C3, 55 D4
Gomphoi 53 C2
Gonnos 53 D2
Gortyn 54 F2
Gytheion 55 C2

Halikarnassos 59 D3
Hellespont, strait 57 D3
Hephaistia 57 C2
Herakleia 59 D3
Hierapytna 54 G2

Ialysos 59 E2
Iasos 59 D3
Idyma 59 E3
Ieropotamos, r. 54 F2
Ikaria, i. 11 E2, 59 C3
Imbros, i. 57 C3
Iolkos 11 C3, 53 D2
Ionian Islands 10 A3
Ionian Sea 10 B2, 54 A3
Ios, i. 58 B2

Istiala 53 E1
Ithaka 10 B3
Ithaka, i. 54 A4

Kalamas, r. 52 B2
Kallipoli 59 E2
Kalydon 54 B4
Kalymnos, i. 59 C2
Kameiros 59 D2
Karpathos, i. 11 E1
Karystos 58 A4
Kassope 52 B2
Kato Zakro 11 E1, 54 H2
Keletron 53 C3
Keos, i. 11 D2
Kephallenia, i. 10 B3, 54 A4
Kephisos, r. 11 C3
Keramos 59 D3
Kerkineon 53 D2
Kerkyra 52 A2
Kerkyra, i. 10 A3, 52 A2
Klazomenai 59 C4
Knidos 59 D2
Knossos 11 D1, 54 G2
Kolophon 59 D4
Koroneia 55 C4
Koropi 53 E2
Koryphasion 11 B2
Kos 59 D2
Kos, i. 11 E2, 59 D2
Krisa 55 C4
Kydonia 11 C1, 54 F2
Kythera 55 C2
Kythera, i. 11 C2, 55 D2
Kythnos, i. 11 D2

Larisa 11 C3, 53 D2
Laureion 55 D2
Lebedos 59 C4
Lemnos, i. 11 D3, 57 C2
Lerna 11 C2, 55 C3
Lesbos, i. 11 E3, 57 C2
Leukas 52 B1
Leukas, i. 10 B3, 52 B1
Leuktra 55 D4
Levena 54 F1
Lindos 11 F2, 59 E2
Lissos 54 E2
Lycaonia, Gulf of 55 C2

Macedonia, d. 11 B4
Mallia 54 G2
Malthi 11 B2
Mantineia 55 C3
Marathon 11 C3, 55 D4
Mediterranean Sea 11 C1
Megara 55 D4
Melene 57 D2
Melos, i. 11 D2, 58 A2

Messene 54 B3
Methone 53 D3
Methymna 57 D2
Metropolis 53 C2
Miletos 11 E2, 59 D3
Mirtoan Sea 55 D2
Mycenae 11 C2, 55 C3
Mykonos, i. 58 B3
Myndos 59 D3
Mytilene 57 D2

Naupaktos 54 B4
Nauplia 11 C2, 55 C3
Naxos, i. 11 D2, 58 B3
Neapolis 56 B3
Nekromanteion of Ephrya 52 B2
Nemea 55 C3
Nestos, r. 11 D4, 56 B4
Nikopolis 52 B2
Notion 59 D4
Nyssa 59 E3

Oiniadai 54 B4
Olympia 11 B2, 54 B3
Olympos, Mount 11 C4, 53 D3
Olynthos 53 E3
Orchomenos 11 C3, 55 C4
Orchomenos 55 C3

Pagasai 53 D2
Panionion 59 D3
Paros, i. 11 D2, 58 B3
Passandra 57 D2
Pazarköy 57 E2
Peiraieus 55 D3
Peirasia 53 D2
Pella 53 D3
Peloponnese, d. 11 B2
Pergamon 57 E2
Phaistos 11 D1, 54 F2
Phalasarna 54 E2
Pheria 53 D2
Philippi 56 B4
Phoenike 52 B2
Phokaia 11 E3
Pindos Mountains 11 B3, 52 B3
Pinios, r. 11 C3, 53 D2
Pinios, r. 54 B3
Plataia 55 D4
Poliochni 57 C2
Poros, i. 55 D3
Poteidaia 53 E3
Priene 59 D3
Propontis, sea (Sea of Marmara) 11 E4, 57 E3
Pydna 53 D3

Pylos 11 B2, 54 B3
Pyrrha 57 D2

Rheneia, i. 58 B3
Rhodes 59 E2
Rhodes, i. 11 F2, 59 D2

Salamis, i. 55 D3
Samos 59 C3
Samos, i. 11 E2, 59 C3
Samothrace, i. 11 D4, 57 C3
Sardis 59 E4
Saronic Gulf 55 D3
Semani, r. 52 A3
Sesklo 11 C3
Shkumbini, r. 52 B4
Sigeion 57 D2
Sikyon 55 C3
Skyros, 56 B1
Skyros, i. 11 D3
Smyrna 59 D4
Sounion 55 E3
Sparta 11 C2, 55 C3
Sporades, Northern, isls. 11 C3, 56 A2
Sporades, Southern, isls. 11 E2, 59 C3
Stageira 56 A3
Stratos 53 C3
Strymon, r. 56 A3

Tanagra 55 D4
Tegea 55 C3
Tenos 58 B3
Tenos, i. 11 D2, 58 B3
Teos 59 C4
Thasos, i. 11 D4, 56 D3
Thebes 11 C3, 55 D4
Thera 58 B2
Thera, i. 11 D2, 58 B2
Thermaic Gulf 53 D3
Thermopylai 11 C3, 53 D1
Thespiai 55 D4
Thessaloniki 53 D3
Thessaly, d. 11 C3
Thrace, d. 11 D4
Thracian Sea 57 C3
Tiryns 11 C2, 55 C3
Troizen 55 D3
Troy 11 E3, 57 D2

Vapheio 11 C2
Vergina 53 D3

Xanthi 11 D4

Zakynthos, i. 10 B2, 54 A3

Index